Second Edition

Defending the Spread Offense

John Rice

ISBN: 978-1-60679-081-6
Library of Congress Control Number: 2010920634
Cover design: Brenden Murphy
Text design: Bean Creek Studio
Front cover photo: Joe Robbins/USP

Coaches Choice
P.O. Box 1828
Monterey, CA 93942
www.coacheschoice.com

Dedication

To my Lord and Savior Jesus Christ. Words cannot explain my gratitude for your continuous blessings and grace. Thank you for loving me when I was yet a sinner, taking my place on the cross, and loving me though I continually fall short. I hope my effort within these pages glorifies you, Lord. Guide me in my decisions to come, that I may glorify you with my actions. Amen.

To my wife Mireya, daughters Erica, Emily, and Emma, and my son John Jr.—you are my treasure and the Lord's greatest blessing! Thank you for sacrifices you make and support for my coaching career.

Foreword

Football is a remarkable game. In any given week, a variety of different coaching philosophies and approaches to the game are on display at all competitive levels—from youth leagues to the NFL.

In a very real sense, the game is constantly evolving. New systems. New schemes. New coaches. New points of emphasis. Perhaps no single change in recent years has impacted the game more than the spread offense.

It often appears that every team in football has incorporated some form of the spread into its offensive attack. With its focus on speed, creating space, and fast pace, the spread has brought both excitement to the game and high anxiety to defensive coordinators.

Defending the Spread Offense (Second Edition) was developed as a tool for coaches who want to be fully prepared to address the issues involved in defending the spread. The concepts, principles, and ideas that it provides are spot-on. The book also reinforces John's position as one of the truly innovative authors in the game.

Defending the Spread Offense (Second Edition) is an exceptional resource for coaches at all competitive levels—whether they are being exposed to the need to be able to defend the spread offense for a first time or are simply looking for new ideas for stopping this offensive juggernaut. Ultimately, John's ideas will help you to become a better coach, just as they have helped me over the years.

— Jeff Steinberg
Head Football Coach
Santiago High School
Corona, CA

Contents

Dedication 3

Foreword 4

Preface 6

Chapter

1   Basketball on Grass 7

2   Understanding the Philosophy of the Spread Offense 9

3   Formulating a Defensive Strategy 17

4   Attacking Various Pass Protection Schemes 25

5   The 4-2-5 Nickel Versus the Spread Offense 32

6   The 3-3-5 Nickel Versus the Spread Offense 58

7   The Dime Package Versus the Spread Offense 76

8   The 3-2-6 Dime Versus the Spread Offense 109

9   The 4-3 Defense Versus the Spread Offense 133

10   46 Nickel Versus the Spread Offense 142

11   Even-Front Strategies Versus an Empty Backfield 155

12   Odd-Front Strategies Versus an Empty Backfield 176

13   Fusing Bracket Coverage and Pressure Concepts
      Versus the Spread Offense 193

About the Author 203

Preface

This book is meant to serve as a reference. It is not an all-inclusive defensive system or a 'how-to" manual. My purpose is not to advocate one particular strategy or devote too much space to individual techniques, but rather to educate the reader as to the myriad of strategies available to the defensive coordinator when defending the spread offense. Hopefully, you may be able to adapt something within these pages and incorporate it into your scheme. Purposely, no specific alignments appear within the diagrams because within your scheme, you may like to play particular players at certain depths (and widths or shades). For instance, you may prefer off-man pass technique rather than either press man or catch-and-trail man technique, and for that reason, I have not designated defensive position alignments within the diagrams, in order to let the individual coach "fill in" those designations. The same goes for the alignments and reads of the defensive linemen. You may prefer to always play a weakside defensive end in a loose 5 or 7 technique on passing downs. Maybe you like playing double 2 techniques in the even front. For this reason, I've left it up to you to decide what is best for your defense. Good luck.

1

Basketball on Grass

Occasionally referred to as "basketball on grass," the spread offense is a fast-paced offensive system that spreads the field with four and five receivers. Typically executed with the quarterback in a shotgun formation, the spread offense attempts to spread the field horizontally and to distribute the ball to the four- and five-receiver sets.

In the spread offense, the offense often lines up with relatively wide splits between the linemen, in order to create multiple avenues of open space that the passing game, as well as the running game, can exploit. These expanded gaps force the defense to spread itself thin horizontally, which makes it somewhat difficult for it to do its job effectively.

In a very real sense, spread offenses have affected the ways that teams are playing defense. Because the offense puts up to six athletes in space, defenses are forced to get as much speed as possible on the field to try to slow down spread attacks. As a result, teams are employing smaller, faster defensive players to cover more of the field.

The difficulty of defending the spread offense is exacerbated by the fact that many different versions of the spread exist. Some schools (e.g., Texas Tech, Oklahoma, Missouri, Tulsa, etc.) employ a pass-oriented version of the spread. Other schools (e.g., United States Naval Academy, Nevada, Oregon, Georgia Tech, etc.), on the other hand, feature a run-oriented spread attack to disrupt defenses. The variety of spread offenses requires defenses to make adjustments in what they have to do each week—an imperative that makes their jobs even more difficult to do successfully.

Truth be known, no magic defenses exist. If they did, every team would employ one of them, and no offense would score. What is known, however, is that certain fundamental defensive concepts and principles—when properly applied—can help slow down the spread. *Defending the Spread Offense (Second Edition)* details those precepts and reviews how they can be employed to defend the spread. Collectively, they provide an effective tool that coaches can use to defend this often flourishing offensive system until an innovative new defense is designed to catch up with and stop the spread.

2

Understanding the Philosophy of the Spread Offense

This chapter covers the common philosophical beliefs that are at the heart of the spread offense.

Spreading the Field Through Formations and Motion

The primary aim of spreading the field using formations with three, four, and five receivers is to make the defense cover every receiver, thereby removing run defenders from the box and opening running lanes. By using spread formations, the offense is hoping to force a linebacker, usually a run defender, to play in space against a more athletic receiver, creating a mismatch. A defender with the primary responsibility of deep pass coverage is not as effective in stopping the run. Spread formations make it easier for the quarterback to read the coverage alignment, and harder for the defense to disguise their coverage. It is also very hard for defenses to blitz from the secondary without showing their intent to do so. Spread formations also use motion by the back or a receiver to help the quarterback recognize coverage, i.e., zone or man. When defenses start using man coverage, it forces them to show who has man-to-man responsibility, and who may be blitzing.

"Take What You Give Us" Philosophy

When the defense is crowding the box and using pressing man-to-man techniques on the receivers, the offense should throw vertical to get them to back off. When the defense sits back and plays zone, the offense should play "dink and dunk." In other words, they should just play catch and try to get upfield between the zone defenders.

Running the Football Versus Appropriate Numbers

If a defense decides to play with two safeties, an offense using a four-receiver set can create a favorable match-up (five blockers for five defenders) for a successful running play. If five defenders align in the box, either with four down linemen and one linebacker, or three down linemen with two linebackers, the offense has the ability to change the play at the line and call a run. Diagram 2-1 illustrates changing the play to a quarterback draw.

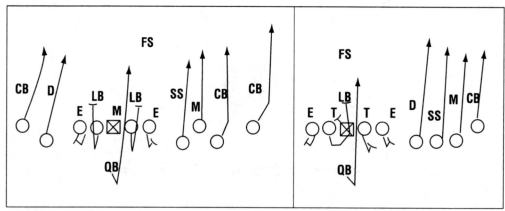

Diagram 2-1. Changing the play to a quarterback draw

Passing the Football Versus Appropriate Numbers

If a defense decides to play with six defenders in the box (four down linemen with two inside linebackers, or three down linemen with three linebackers), the offense can create a favorable situation for a pass play. If the offense sends four receivers out in the pass route versus a man-free scheme, they will likely get a good match-up versus one of three receivers (Diagram 2-2). If the offense has five wideouts, they will get man coverage on all five if the safety picks up the fifth receiver. At this point, all they have to do is hit the one of the five who is without safety help (Diagram 2-3).

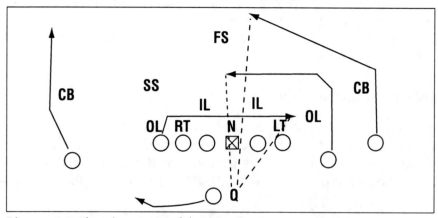

Diagram 2-2. Throwing to one of three receivers

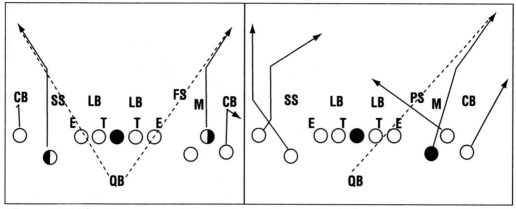

Diagram 2-3. Throwing to one of five receivers without safety help

Stretching the Defense Vertically with the Deep Passing Game

Many spread offenses try to put a vertical stretch on the defense, taking the top off of the coverage in throwing the ball either behind or in front of the secondary. Perimeter defenders worried about the deep pass are usually less effective in stopping the run.

Throwing to Uncovered Receivers

Another key advantage to the spread is that by using four or five receivers, defenders are forced to cover all of the receivers. Common spread philosophy dictates that a defense must commit one defender for every receiver in the formation, or the offense will throw to the uncovered man, which often means that a linebacker must leave the box and cover a wide receiver or slot player, weakening the defense versus a running play (Diagram 2-4).

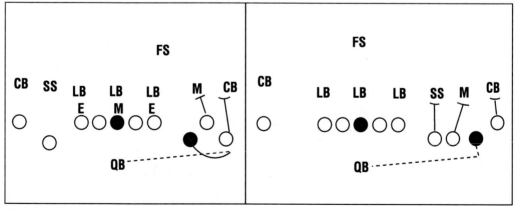

Diagram 2-4. Throwing to uncovered receivers

Create Big Plays Versus the Blitz

Spread offense philosophy entails that if a defense chooses to blitz them, they will attack the blitz with hot reads, sight adjustments by the receivers, screens, and draws. Many spread offenses have the philosophy of "recognize the blitz, protect the blitz, and attack the blitz." They believe that by adopting this blitz philosophy, sooner or later, the offense is going to get a big play. They expect to make big plays versus the blitz. Diagram 2-5 illustrates a funnel screen to a wide receiver versus a blitz.

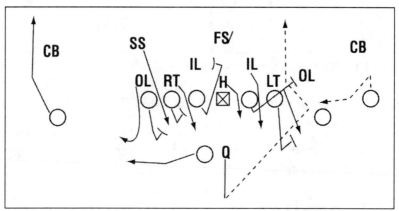

Diagram 2-5. Funnel screen

In summary, the spread offense attempts to dominate the defense by:

- Spreading the field by formation motion
- Using audibles to run versus five defenders in the box, or pass versus six defenders in the box
- Stretching the defense vertically with the deep pass
- Throwing to uncovered receivers
- Creating big plays versus the blitz

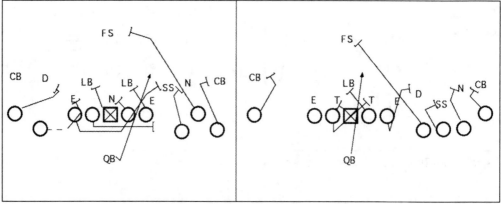

Diagram 2-6. A common audible versus four or five in the box is a quarterback trap or counter.

In addition, the defenses who prepare most of the season for a two-back offense have a limited amount of time to prepare during a practice week to defend the spread offense. Diagrams 2-6 to 2-11 include some of the common audibles used by the spread offense.

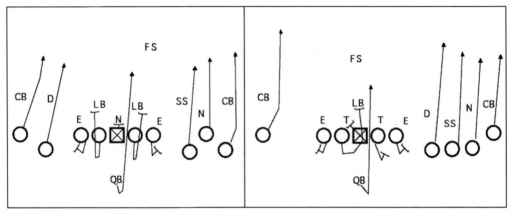

Diagram 2-7. A common audible versus four or five in the box is a quarterback draw.

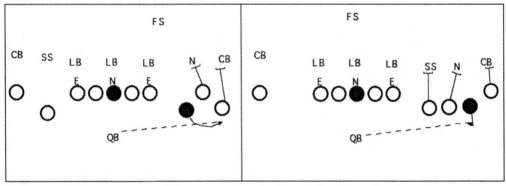

Diagram 2-8. A common audible versus six in the box with a free safety is to throw to the uncovered receiver on a quick hitch or bubble screen.

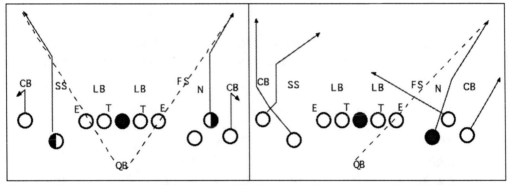

Diagram 2-9. A common audible versus six in the box without a free safety is to take advantage of a personnel mismatch, such as a safety or fifth defensive back on a wideout.

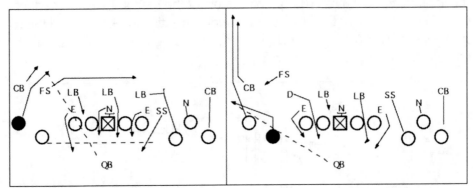

Diagram 2-10. A common audible to seven in the box when a blitz is likely is to throw a backside slant to take advantage of the one-on-one match-up. Another option is to throw "hot" off of a blitzing defensive back aligned on a slot receiver. You can also throw to the slot before the blitz adjuster can get to the quick out.

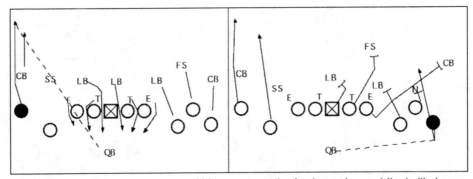

Diagram 2-11. Other common audibles to seven in the box when a blitz is likely are fades and wide-receiver screens.

Diagram 2-12 summarizes the common spread offense audibles from four-wide receiver (one-back) formations.

Diagram 2-13 summarizes the common spread offense audibles from five-wide receiver (empty-backfield) formations.

Diagram 2-14 shows examples of the most common offensive formations used in the spread offense. All of the formations can be run with the quarterback under the center or in the shotgun.

Some common running plays used in the spread offense are:

- Dart/wrap
- Inside/outside zone
- Counter trey
- Fullback and quarterback trap

- Jet sweep
- Speed option
- Shovel pass
- Fullback and quarterback draw

Defensive Alignment to 1 back with 4 wideouts

	4 in the box 3-1-7 quarter	5 in the box 3-2-6 dime 4-1-6 dime	6 in the box 3-3-5 nickel 4-2-5 nickel	7 in the box (blitz coming) 4-3-4 (43 defense) 5-2-4 (50 defense) 3-4-4 (3-4 defense)
Common Spread Offense responses to defensive alignments	Audible to: inside zone dive counter trey trap jet sweep	Audible to: outside zone veer dive counter trey trap jet sweep	vs. Free Safety: throw to uncovered receiver (hitch/bubble screen)	throw hot; use sight adustments by receivers on blitzes
			vs cover 0: find mismatch & (LB on wide out)	audible to: fade vs. press man slant vs. off man hitch vs. off man WR screens (rocket, middle, jailbreak) draw

Diagram 2-12. Common spread offense audibles from four wide receiver (one back) formations.

Defensive Alignment to 5 wideouts (Empty)

	4 in the box 3-1-7 quarter	5 in the box 3-2-6 dime 4-1-6 dime	6 in the box 3-3-5 nickel 4-2-5 nickel	7 in the box (blitz coming) 4-3-4 (43 defense) 5-2-4 (50 defense) 3-4-4 (3-4 defense)
Diagram				
Spread Offense response to defensive alignment	Audible to: QB counter QB draw	Audible to: QB counter QB draw	vs. Free Safety: throw to uncovered receiver (hitch or bubble screen)	throw hot; use sight adustments by receivers on blitzes
			vs cover 0: find mismatch & (LB on wide out)	audible to: fade/slant/screen/draw

Diagram 2-13. Common spread offense audibles from five-wide receiver (empty backfield) formations

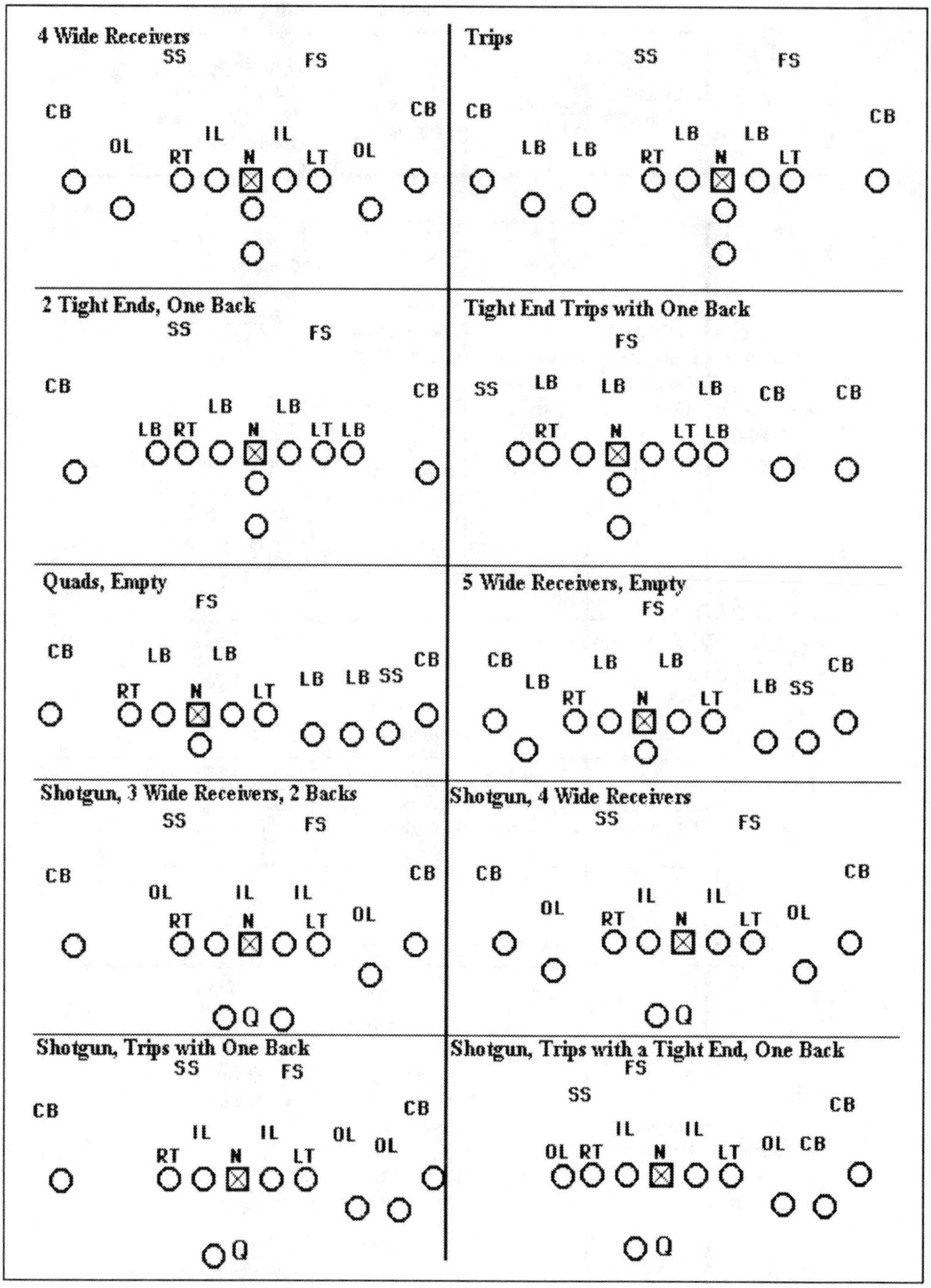
4 Wide Receivers
SS FS
CB CB
IL IL
OL RT N LT OL
Trips
SS FS
CB CB
LB LB
LB LB RT N LT
2 Tight Ends, One Back
SS FS
CB CB
LB LB
LB RT N LT LB
Tight End Trips with One Back
FS
SS LB LB LB CB CB
RT N LT LB
Quads, Empty
FS
CB LB LB CB
LB LB SS
RT N LT
5 Wide Receivers, Empty
FS
CB LB LB CB
LB
RT N LT LB SS
Shotgun, 3 Wide Receivers, 2 Backs
SS FS
CB CB
OL IL IL
RT N LT OL
Q
Shotgun, 4 Wide Receivers
SS FS
CB CB
IL IL
OL RT N LT OL
Q
Shotgun, Trips with One Back
SS FS
CB CB
IL IL OL OL
RT N LT
Q
Shotgun, Trips with a Tight End, One Back
FS
SS CB
IL IL
OL RT N LT OL CB
Q
Diagram 2-14. Commonly used formations in the spread offense

3

Formulating a Defensive Strategy

Once a solid understanding of common spread offense philosophy is achieved, some general principles should be considered when preparing to defend a spread offense. The following considerations should help in the planning and execution of a game plan versus the spread offense.

- Play the fastest players on defense. If necessary, play five, six, or seven defensive backs. If necessary, play with six linebackers. Get the quickest, most athletic defenders on the field.
- If possible, play the same 11 personnel versus the spread and minimize personnel changes. Thus, the offense can't get a read on the defense. For instance, don't replace one or two linebackers with defensive backs in the nickel or dime package if it's not necessary. Any nickel or dime scheme can be run with base personnel, if the athletes are good enough.
- Stop the running game first, with the fewest number of defenders in the box as possible. If able to stop the run with five in the box, the defense is at a tremendous advantage. If unable to stop them from running the ball with five, then play with six in the box.
- If able to create pressure on the quarterback rushing four and dropping seven into coverage, the defense is at a tremendous advantage. This can be done by rushing all four down linemen in an even front, or from a 3-2 alignment and sending one of the linebackers. Mix up the looks.
- If able to effectively defend the spread offense dropping eight into coverage every down, therefore eliminating the big pass play while not allowing big runs or sustained offensive possessions, the defense is in the driver's seat.

- If able to load the line of scrimmage with eight defenders (therefore taking the run away and making the offense one-dimensional) without getting beat with the deep pass, the defense is in the driver's seat.
- Disrupt the rhythm of the offense. Regardless of the defensive alignment (50, 43, etc.), don't give the offense accurate pre-snap reads. Force the linemen, quarterback, and receivers to make post-snap reads and sight adjustments under pressure. Find out if the quarterback is waiting for a call from the press box, where the coaches wait for the defense to line up, and then send a play down to the sideline, which is signaled in to the quarterback. Wait until the play is signaled in, and then stem the defensive front occasionally as a change-up. Or, show the same defensive alignment every play until the play is signaled in, and then make alignment adjustments. Move defensive backs up and back, or in and out before the play is signaled in. The defense can also line up in the same defensive alignment but must be able to play various pass coverages after the ball is snapped.

Diagram 3-1 details a defensive-ready list that illustrates how to use the aforementioned principles when formulating a game plan.

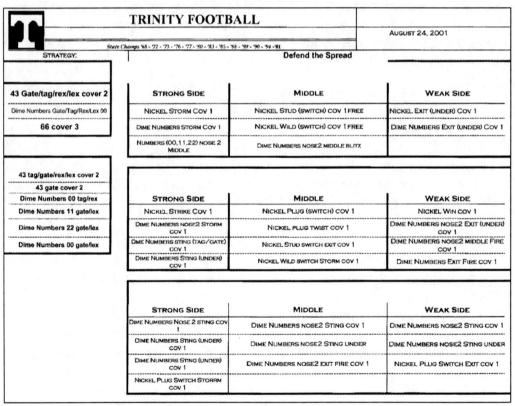

Diagram 3-1. Defense-ready list vs. spread offense

Have Multiple Adjustments to Formations and Motion

Offensive coordinators will use motion and multiple formations early in a game to identify defensive alignments and coverage. If limited to one defensive adjustment to a particular offensive formation, the offense will have an answer for it very quickly because they will have scouted it in previous weeks, practiced against that one adjustment all week, and be confident in their execution. Using more than one alignment for each offensive formation prevents the offense from operating in rhythm, especially if they line up expecting to see a certain defensive alignment, and the defense is not lined up as they have been shown all week in practice. Have *at least* two defensive adjustments for every formation.

Diagrams 3-2 and 3-3 illustrate two different alignments of a 4-3 defense versus a three-wide receiver, one-tight end formation common to spread offenses.

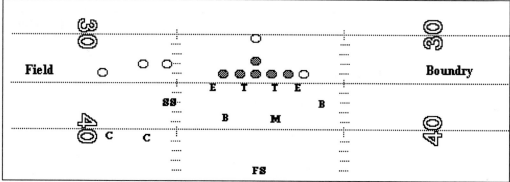

Diagram 3-2. 4-3 defense versus three wide receivers and one tight end

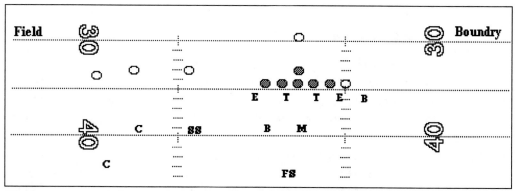

Diagram 3-3. 4-3 defense versus three wide receivers and one tight end

Diagrams 3-4 and 3-5 illustrate two different alignments of a 4-3 defense versus a two-wide receiver, two-tight ends formation common to spread offenses.

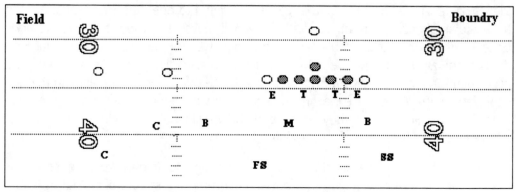

Diagram 3-4. 4-3 defense versus two wide receivers and two tight ends

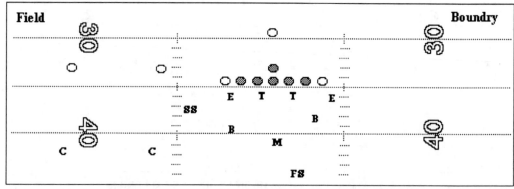

Diagram 3-5. 4-3 defense versus two wide receivers and two tight ends

Teaching Progression/Installation of Adjustments

It is beneficial to practice multiple adjustments to specific spread formations during seven-on-seven passing contests in the summer so that when the season begins, defenders are comfortable and confident in aligning and executing these assignments. It may be helpful to use the "part-part-whole concept." In the early summer seven-on-seven contests, play one defensive adjustment per formation per game. Perhaps play the adjustment for two games before adding the next adjustment. Then, during the next game, play a second (different) adjustment. Play this adjustment until the players show efficiency, and then progress to playing both adjustments, perhaps one each half. Play only the third adjustment in a game or two until the defenders are good at it. Finally, in every game thereafter, play all three adjustments. During the season, script pass skeleton so that all three adjustments can be made at any time.

Jam Receivers at Different Levels on Pass Plays

When defending the spread offense, disrupt the offense's rhythm by either putting pressure on the quarterback or jamming the receivers. Disrupting receivers' routes by physically rerouting them is a key to disrupting the timing of the three-step game. Jamming receivers at different depths in their routes may help prevent the receivers from anticipating a jam and using a counter move. Among the ways to vary the disruption of the receiver's timing are to use press-man technique off the line of scrimmage, catch-and-trail technique at five yards, and a squat-corner technique in a two-deep coverage. Begin teaching these different techniques in seven on seven contests in the summer. Use the same teaching progressions as previously described for defensive adjustments. Begin by only jamming receivers at the line of scrimmage. Next, progress to jamming them at five yards, mixing in a squat-corner technique. Follow up by using all three techniques in the later summer passing contests, which will build confidence in the defenders' ability to reroute receivers, and disrupt the timing of the passing game.

Be Prepared for the Pace of the No-Huddle Strategy

One way to simulate the pace of the no-huddle offense is to use a two-huddle offense in which one unit runs a play, and then the second offense walks up to the line of scrimmage as the first play ends. The first string quarterback should take all the snaps to provide continuity. The key is to keep the offensive linemen and receivers fresh, while conditioning the defense. This type of strategy for simulating the pace of the no-huddle should be practiced in the summer prior to the season. Defenders must be in excellent physical condition to be effective against the no-huddle spread offense.

Decide how to handle communicating the defensive calls in this fast-paced situation. The defense will get badly burned if it doesn't mix the calls and plays just one scheme. The offense is trying to do a couple things: first, disrupt the defense from communicating with each other and the coordinator, and second, prevent the defense from using personnel groupings, like nickel- or dime-package personnel.

The defense can choose to respond in several ways. The first is to signal the defensive call to the entire defense. In this case, everyone must know the defensive signals. The second is to signal to one defender and have him relay the call to the other defenders. A variation of this play is to signal a call to two defenders, one from the front and one from the secondary. A third way to handle the no-huddle is to use defensive wristbands, which have the defensive calls color-coded for easy recognition. For example, use three or four colors preceding a number. For instance, straight zones may be coded blue, stunts are red, and zone pressure is yellow. If a coach signaled/called, "Red 7," the defenders would be able to quickly look to the red-coded calls and only have a small number of defenses to look at, instead of grouping all the defensive calls together by name. One way of avoiding the time-consuming task of completely restructuring the wristbands weekly in order to prevent opponents from stealing the signals is to just change the color-code designations. For example, during week one, reds could be the key for blitzes, and for week two, the key for straight zone. Thus, rotate the color scheme weekly, and avoid having to come up with different calls every week.

❑ *Take away an opponent's best receiver by alignment, coverage, or both*

Identify the opponent's best player and double-cover him. If they have players who can beat the defenders one-on-one, give them a heavy dose of double-bracket coverage. Remember to teach the defense the coverage weakness when using double-coverage.

❑ *Unless your athletes are superior to the offense's, defend the spread with a blend of coverage and pressure—"mix it up"*

Pick the spots for sending five, six, or seven rushers. Take calculated gambles, based on sound scouting of the opponent. Self-scouting will allow coaches to recognize their own defensive habits and, if necessary, alter them so that the offense will have a more difficult time exploiting a tendency. Drop five, six, seven, eight, or nine into pass coverage.

Know the Opposing Offensive Coordinator's Philosophy

Determine if the offensive coordinator for a spread team would rather run or pass the ball if given his choice. On occasion, the defensive coaches can use this information to their advantage. Generally, offensive coordinators running the spread will fit into one of three categories:

• They are in the spread to throw the ball. They will throw it on any down, from anywhere on the field, against any coverage, against eight or nine in pass coverage. In general, they believe that the spread dictates to the defense, and not vice versa. They will throw a run in occasionally to keep the linebackers honest. Their run blocking will not be great, but they will usually be good at pass protection.

• They pass to set up the run. They use formations to stretch the defense horizontally and to create running lanes. If given the chance, they will run the ball until the defense stops the run.

• They will take what is given to them. If you have five in the box, they will check to a run every time. They are patient enough to run the ball down the field if that's what is given to them.

After scouting the opponent, attempt to categorize the opposing offensive coordinator and then scheme to take away what that particular spread offense does best. Challenge spread offenses to do the opposite of what they want to do. For example, when facing an offense whose coordinator wants to throw the ball 70 percent of the time, make it as difficult as possible for him to do that. Drop seven, eight, or nine into coverage and dare them to run it. See if they are willing to drive 80 yards by running the ball 15 times. Most coordinators who want to throw the ball aren't patient enough to run in this situation. Sometime during a drive, they will throw the ball versus a five-man front because of pride or impatience, which is when they may throw an interception with eight or nine in pass coverage. Likewise, if a team has a great running back, take him out of the game and dare them to throw by playing seven or eight in the box. Are they good enough to march 80 yards down the field with the short-passing game? If so, mix it up by showing six and seven man fronts, and then drop eight into coverage.

It is much more difficult to prepare for a spread offense when an opposing offensive coordinator is patient enough to take what you give them. In this case, it may be best to mix up the fronts, pressure, and coverage, and try to prevent accurate pre-snap reads. Make them earn every yard. Don't give them any cheap touchdowns. Sometimes, versus a disciplined offense that will run or pass with equal effectiveness, try to slow them down, and make them drive the length of the field.

❑ *Analyze and understand the pass protection scheme of your opponent*

If the coach chooses to use pressure (more than a four-man rush), he must understand and utilize the specific ways to attack common pass-protection schemes. An example of commonly used pass protections and methods of attacking them are discussed in later chapters.

Sending one more than the offense can block in any protection scheme is the most direct way to beat a protection. Another way is to identify their weakest pass protector, who may or may not be a lineman. If a lineman is their weak link, line up the best pass rusher against him. Consider using stunts if he isn't particularly good at switching off. When facing a big-on-big protection or slide protection with a back blocking, and the back is the weak link, send a defender who can beat him on every play. Align the best rusher so that the back used in protection, according to his rules, must block the best rusher. Creating mismatches is a major key to defending the spread offense.

Sending four rushers to the weakside causes problems versus the spread. When in an even front, play a 1 technique and a 5 technique, and send both a linebacker and a defensive back. The offense can counter by either sliding the protection to your blitz and using the back as a fourth man, or they could try and fan the center to the weakside to handle the fourth rusher. However, by playing an odd front, and causing the center to block the nose, the offense is forced to block four rushers versus only three protectors (weakside guard and tackle, along with the back.)

❑ *Be willing to adopt an "it depends" philosophy when determining how to adjust to different formations*

Don't be rigid. KEEP AN OPEN MIND. Don't be locked into a specific adjustment versus a specific formation. Analyze why a team gets into a particular formation in a particular situation. Many spread teams get into a trips formation to force three defenders to commit to the pass, and then they run the ball. If the opponent gets into a trips formation primarily to run the ball, don't commit three defenders to the trips side. Make them throw the bubble screen to the uncovered man, instead of being forced to play three-on-three against a trips formation. Also, the defense is in a favorable position if it can handle the backside receiver one-on-one, because an extra defender can be committed to the run. If the offense is better on the single-cut side, then walk a linebacker half the distance and allow the corner to back up a bit and defend against the deep pass. However, this adjustment will create a weakness versus the run. All of these factors should be considered when making a game plan.

❑ *Anticipate the offensive coordinator's adjustments to the game plan, and have a countermove for each strategy the offense employs*

Be ready to adjust if the offense forces the defense out of the game plan on the first drive of the game. Try something until it works, go with it until they adjust, and then find something else that works. Have these contingencies built into the game plan. Prepare the defenders to adjust as needed. Never panic. View the game as a chess match. In other words, be flexible. Have the tools (adjustments) built into the defensive game plan to answer whatever the offense does. For example, be able to drop eight into pass coverage, or load the line of scrimmage when the situation calls for it. Or, be able to double-cover receivers, and have a zone-pressure package.

Attacking Various Pass Protection Schemes

In order to plan effective blitzes from the nickel and dime package, an understanding of offensive pass protection schemes is essential. Four of the most common pass protection schemes are:

- Big-on-big protection
- Slide protection
- Turnback protection
- Fan protection

Diagrams 4-1 to 4-12 illustrate examples of each of these four protection schemes. An explanation of how to attack each protection scheme accompanies each diagram.

Big-on-Big Protection

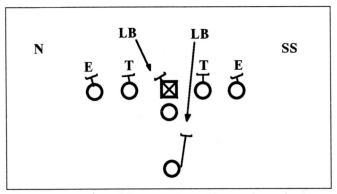

Diagram 4-1. Big-on-big protection without a hot scheme

Big-on-big protection is a commonly used protection scheme in high school football. In this scheme, offensive linemen are assigned man-for-man protection versus particular offensive linemen. This example is a one-back set versus a 4-2-5 nickel defense. The four defensive linemen, two linebackers, and the nickel and strong safety are all threats to rush the passer. The guards and tackles will be assigned to the defensive linemen in front of them, and the center would block a blitzing linebacker in one of the A-gaps. The back would be responsible for a second inside blitzing linebacker. Diagram 4-2 illustrates how to attack big-on-big protection that does not use a "hot" scheme. The weakness of this protection scheme is against an outside blitz from the strong safety and/or nickel. The offense is outnumbered, and the outside blitzers are unaccounted for.

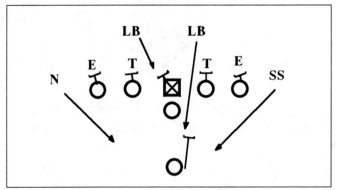

Diagram 4-2. Attacking big-on-big protection that does not use a "hot" scheme

Diagram 4-3 shows an example of big-on-big protection using a hot scheme with a back.

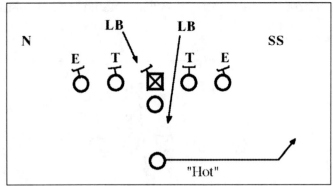

Diagram 4-3. Big-on-big protection using a "hot" scheme with a back

If the offense identifies the inside linebacker as hot and he blitzes, the back would flair, and the quarterback would dump the ball quickly. Diagram 4-4 illustrates how to attack big-on-big protection that uses a back as a "hot" receiver. The weakness of this protection scheme versus a nickel or dime zone blitz (where the strong safety is responsible for the flat) would negate the effectiveness of the dump pass, because the flat defender would be waiting for the "hot" receiver.

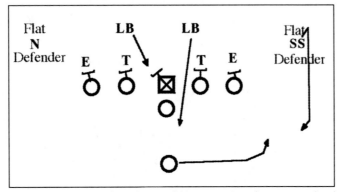

Diagram 4-4. Attacking big-on-big protection that uses a back as a "hot" receiver

Diagram 4-5 illustrates an example of big-on-big protection using a tight end as a "hot" receiver.

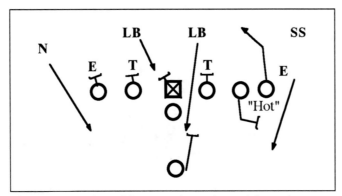

Diagram 4-5. Big-on-big protection using a tight end as a "hot" receiver

If the strongside inside linebacker blitzes against an offense that uses a hot scheme with a tight end, the tight end would simply go to the area vacated by the blitzing linebacker, and the quarterback would dump him the ball. The back would most likely be in a dual-pickup mode, checking for an inside blitz first; and if the inside linebacker showed, he would be responsible for picking him up. The strongside tackle would block the strongside defensive end.

Diagram 4-6 illustrates an example of how to attack big-on-big protection using a tight end as a "hot" receiver. The key to attacking this particular protection scheme is keeping the "hot" receiver (the tight end) on the line of scrimmage by putting a pass defender in his face, and sending an outside blitzer who is unaccounted for. An offensive countermove may be to run a quick fade with the tight end. In both the nickel and the dime package, a safety could be assigned to defend a fade by the tight end in this blitzing situation. Because of the nickel's blitz weakside, the quarterback should have to get rid of the ball quickly. If he hesitates trying to throw to the tight end, the nickel should have time to make a big hit on the passer.

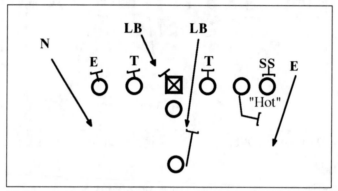

Diagram 4-6. Attacking big-on-big protection that uses a tight end as a "hot" receiver

Slide Protection

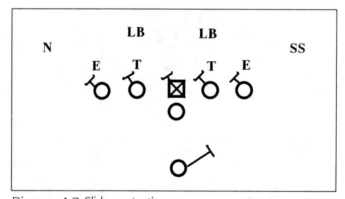

Diagram 4-7. Slide protection

In slide protection, (frequently employed in the quick passing game), the linemen are assigned to protect a pre-determined gap, and slide-step to protect that gap. The remaining back steps opposite the sliding linemen and is responsible for blocking any rusher who shows from the outside. Unlike big-on-big protection, the offensive linemen in slide protection are not assigned to block a particular defender. Rather, they are assigned to block any defender who shows in the gap assigned to them.

Diagram 4-8 provides an example of how to attack slide protection. The key to effectively attacking slide protection is to disrupt the timing of the pass receivers and send an extra outside rusher to the side of the slide. In Diagram 4-8, the nickel is blitzing. Since a three-step drop or less is used with this protection, the quarterback must be made to hesitate either by jamming the receivers at the line of scrimmage, or by using a catch technique (where the defensive backs jam the receivers at five yards.)

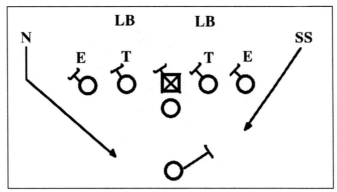

Diagram 4-8. Attacking slide protection

Turnback Protection

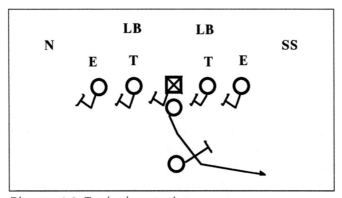

Diagram 4-9. Turnback protection

Turnback protection is often used when the quarterback is rolling out to pass. The offensive linemen will block back, away from the direction of the roll. The offensive linemen are responsible for any rusher showing in their gap. Their assignment is to make the rusher go around them, away from the quarterback's roll. The back is assigned to handle any outside rush to the side of the roll.

Diagram 4-10 provides an example of how to attack turnback protection. Attacking turnback protection is as easy as sending an extra outside pass rusher away from the turnback blocking. In this case, a strong safety blitzing to the rollout side would be unaccounted for versus turnback protection.

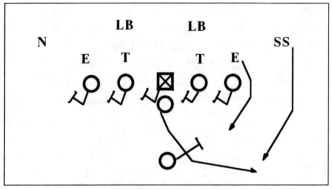

Diagram 4-10. Attacking turnback protection

Fan Protection

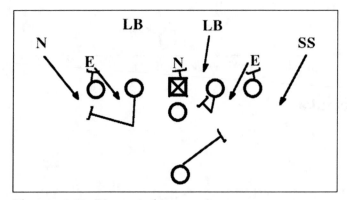

Diagram 4-11. Fan protection

In fan protection, the offensive tackles are assigned to block defensive ends in front of them, and the center is assigned to block the nose. If the scheme uses dual pick-up, the offensive guards, if uncovered, are responsible for picking up a blitzing inside linebacker aligned over them. If the inside linebacker aligned over him does not rush, the guard would fan out and block the outside rusher to his side. The remaining back would block an outside rusher to the side of a blitzing inside linebacker. Fan protection is commonly used against odd fronts when the guards are uncovered.

Diagram 4-12 illustrates an example of how to attack fan protection. Attacking fan protection is as simple as outnumbering the offense. By sending the two inside linebackers, the guards are forced to pick them up, and the back can block only one of the outside rushers. In a nickel or dime scheme, blitzing seven defenders versus a one-back set is an overload the offense cannot handle. They must get rid of the ball quickly or face a sack. Tight man coverage, which denies receivers a free release off the ball, would be used with the blitz.

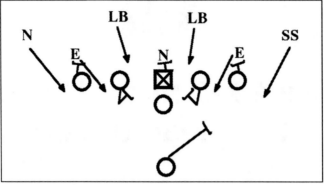

Diagram 4-12. Attacking fan protection

5

The 4-2-5 Nickel Versus the Spread Offense

The History of the 4-2-5 Nickel Versus the Spread Offense

Nickel defenses originated in part as a countermove to the offensive practice of utilizing three-wide receiver offensive formations that spread the defense. The offense did this either by placing running backs in the slots as receivers, by widening tight ends, or by substituting receivers for running backs. With this strategy, offenses could create mismatches by forcing linebackers to align over slot receivers. The two ways defensive coaches avoided these speed mismatches created by three-wide receiver formations were either to play zone pass defense, or to insert a fifth defensive back and align him over the third receiver.

The nickel back, as the fifth defensive back became known, could replace either a defensive lineman or a linebacker. It gave the defense more flexibility, because now that the defense had a defensive back aligned over a third receiver, man-for-man coverage could be played without fear of a third receiver being covered by a linebacker.

The first nickel alignment that was commonly used was a 4-2-5, with four defensive linemen, two linebackers, and five defensive backs. Soon afterwards, offensive strategy evolved, and four- and five-receiver sets began to be utilized. Thereafter, the dime defense was created to counter these offensive sets.

Personnel in the 4-2-5 Nickel

The 4-2-5 nickel is a situational defense that is used in passing situations, and is characterized by inserting a fifth defensive back (called a nickel) for a defensive lineman or a linebacker. Diagram 5-1 illustrates the personnel in the 4-2-5 nickel and their basic alignment.

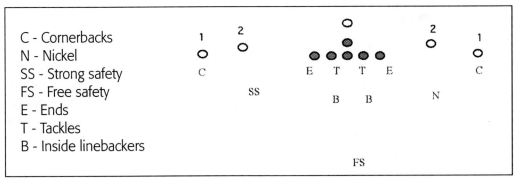

Diagram 5-1. Personnel in the 4-2-5 nickel

Situational uses:

- Against teams that throw in the flats (cover 3 with both flats defended by the strong safety and nickel)
- Against a team that utilizes a three- or four-receiver formation
- Against a team that runs balanced passing formations
- Against a team that, in normal passing situations, shows a tendency to run the ball more than is expected
- Against a team that motions a back to the weakside of a formation

Strengths:

- Four-man rush
- Ability to play zone coverage with five defensive backs
- Strong flat coverage in two-deep or three-deep zone coverage
- Strong outside run support to either side of the formation
- Ability to match speed for speed in a three- or four-receiver set
- Ability to play man coverage with a free safety
- Ability to double-cover one or two receivers in man coverage
- Ability to bring three or four defenders from either side of the formation
- Ability to zone blitz

Weaknesses:

- Three-level flood routes are difficult to defend.
- A six-man front is easier to block than a seven-man front on run plays.

Basic Premise of the 4-2-5 Nickel

The 4-2-5 nickel is characterized by using four down linemen in an even front, two linebackers, and five defensive backs. The fifth defensive back will replace either a down lineman or a linebacker. If a college 4-3 is the base defense, the fifth defensive back will usually replace one of the linebackers. If a 5-2 is the base defense, the fifth defensive back will replace one of the five down linemen. If a 3-4 is the base defense, one of the four linebackers moves to a down lineman, and the fifth defensive back replaces another linebacker.

Diagram 5-2 illustrates the base alignment and technique for each defender in the 4-2-5 nickel, as well as basic responsibilities for run toward the defender, run away, key, and responsibility for drop-back pass. Keep in mind when reading the chart that many alignments are possible for the down linemen and linebackers.

The alignment noted in the chart for the defensive left and right ends is outside eye of the offensive tackle. The technique of the ends is listed as a squeeze technique, similar to the gap-control technique used in a 50 defense, which is because, in some situations, the nickel package will see run, and the ends will have to react accordingly. It is possible to abandon the squeeze technique and adopt a more aggressive pass-rush technique. The ends are responsible for contain rush, unless they are stunting. If backfield run flow is towards them, they are responsible for the off-tackle gap. If flow is away, they are responsible for quarterback bootleg or reverse.

The alignment for the defensive tackles is given as "solid" or head-up on the guard. This recommendation is only meant as one possible alignment. Because shaded alignments are possible, the exact alignment of the defensive tackles should be made according to what is best for that particular defensive call. On any run play, the tackles can play two gaps if they're aligned head-up, or if they are aligned on a shade, they are responsible for the gap to their alignment. On flow away, the defensive tackles are responsible for pursuit and cutback. On a drop-back pass, they rush the passer, either with a pre-determined pass-rush move or a stunt called in the huddle.

The alignment of the linebackers, identified as "stud" and "wild," is listed as either stacked or in a gap. Their exact alignment is flexible. Their technique is listed as "squeeze/hat read," which means they are reading the helmet (hat) of the guard in front of them. Some coaches prefer that the inside linebackers read the backs. The most important point is to be consistent. On flow towards the inside linebacker, they are responsible for defending the gap assigned to them, normally the A or B gap. Usually, the inside linebacker's gap responsibility is the opposite gap assigned the defensive tackle in front of him. So, if the defensive tackle to his side is aligned on the inside shade of the guard, the linebacker will then be responsible for the B gap. If the defensive tackle in front of him is aligned on the outside shade, the inside linebacker will be responsible for the A gap. If flow is away from the inside linebacker, he should not turn his shoulders, but shuffle up and in toward the line of scrimmage. He should maintain backside leverage, overpursue, and be ready to play the cutback.

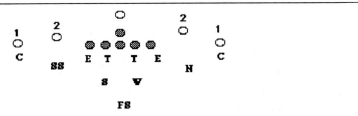

4-2-5 NICKEL FRONT & GAP RESPONSIBILITY CHART

POSITION	ALIGN.	TECHNIQUE	BASIC RESPONSIBILITIES			
			RUN TO	RUN AWAY	KEY	DROPBACK PASS
LEFT END	OUTSIDE EYE OT	SQUEEZE 5 TECH.	OFF TACKLE; IF M/M, FORCE	BOOTLEG REVERSE	BALL TO OT	CONTAIN RUSH OR STUNT
RIGHT END	OUTSIDE EYE OT	SQUEEZE 5 TECH.	OFF TACKLE; IF M/M, FORCE	BOOTLEG REVERSE	BALL TO OT	CONTAIN RUSH OR STUNT
LEFT TACKLE	SOLID OFFENSIVE GUARD	RUSH 2	TWO GAP INSIDE/OUT PLAYER	PURSUIT CUTBACK	BALL TO OG	TWO GAP DEPENDS ON STUNT/BLITZ
RIGHT TACKLE	SOLID OFFENSIVE GUARD	RUSH 2	TWO GAP INSIDE/OUT PLAYER	PURSUIT CUTBACK	BALL TO OG	TWO GAP DEPENDS ON STUNT/BLITZ
STUD ILB	B GAP STRONG OR STACK	SQUEEZE HAT READ	OPPOSITE GAP OF DT IN FRONT	CUTBACK PURSUIT	OG CALL	COVER CALL: MAN/ZONE BLITZ/COMBO
WILD ILB	B GAP WEAK OR STACK	SQUEEZE HAT READ	OPPOSITE GAP OF DT IN FRONT	CUTBACK PURSUIT	OG CALL	COVER CALL: MAN/ZONE BLITZ/COMBO
NICKEL	#2 WEAK OR TRIPS 3 STRONG	MAN/ZONE, BLITZ, OR DBL COVER	IF ZONE, FORCE	CUTBACK PURSUIT	ZONE-UNIT END TO #2; M/M-#2	COVER CALL: MAN/ZONE BLITZ/COMBO
FREE SAFETY	PRE-SNAP 10-12 OFF LOS	MAN-FREE ZONE DBL COVER	INSIDE-OUT SUPPORT	CUTBACK PURSUIT	ONSIDE OG TO QB IN M/M,REC	COVER CALL: MAN/ZONE COVER FOR BLITZER
STRONG SAFETY	2 STRONG OR TRIPS 3 WEAK	MAN/ZONE, BLITZ, OR DBL COVER	IF ZONE, FORCE	CUTBACK PURSUIT	ZONE-UNIT END TO #2; M/M-#2	COVER CALL: MAN/ZONE BLITZ/COMBO
WEAK CORNER	1 STRONG #2 ST TWINS #3 ST TRIPS	MAN/ ZONE OR DOUBLE COVER	PITCH PASS LATE ON SUPPORT	PITCH PASS LATE ON SUPPORT	ZONE-UNIT END TO QB; MAN-REC	COVER CALL: MAN/ZONE OR DBL COVER
STRONG CORNER	1 STRONG #2 WK TWINS #3 WK TRIPS	MAN/ ZONE OR DOUBLE COVER	PITCH PASS LATE ON SUPPORT	PITCH PASS LATE ON SUPPORT	ZONE-UNIT END TO QB; MAN-REC	COVER CALL: MAN/ZONE OR DBL COVER

NOTE: THE ALIGNMENT OF THE DEFENSIVE BACKS ON ASSIGNED RECEIVERS DEPENDS ON A COVER CALL
NOTE: GAP ASSIGNMENTS OF INSIDE BACKERS AND DEFENSIVE TACKLES ARE FLEXIBLE

Diagram 5-2. 4-2-5 nickel front and gap responsibility chart

The strong safety and nickel are defensive backs who are mirrors of each other. The strong safety aligns to the strongside of the formation, over #2. His depth will depend on the pass coverage called. In press-man coverage, he will be up on the line of scrimmage. In zone, he will be off the line of scrimmage. The technique of the strong safety and nickel will depend on the defensive call. They will blitz, play man coverage, or play zone coverage. In zone coverage, the strong safety and nickel will key the unit end (the outer-most player on the line in a three-point stance, either a tight end or tackle) through to the near back. If they are playing man coverage, they will key the receiver lined up in front of them.

The corners align on the #1 receiver to their side, unless trips exist opposite their side, in which case they align over the inside-most receiver. They key the unit end through to the near back. If they are playing man coverage, they will key the receiver lined up in front of them.

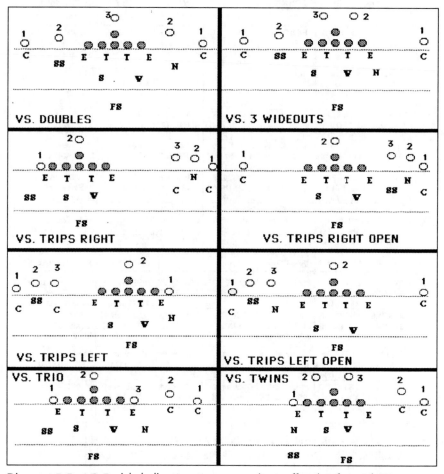

Diagram 5-3. 4-2-5 nickel alignment versus various offensive formations

The free safety's alignment should be between 10 and 12 yards off the line of scrimmage, splitting the distance between the two widest receivers in the offensive formation. In man-free or zone, he should key the guard nearest him, through to the quarterback.

Possible Coverages in the 4-2-5 Nickel

The 4-2-5 nickel defense is flexible. Diagram 5-4 illustrates that a wide variety of coverages may be played from this front.

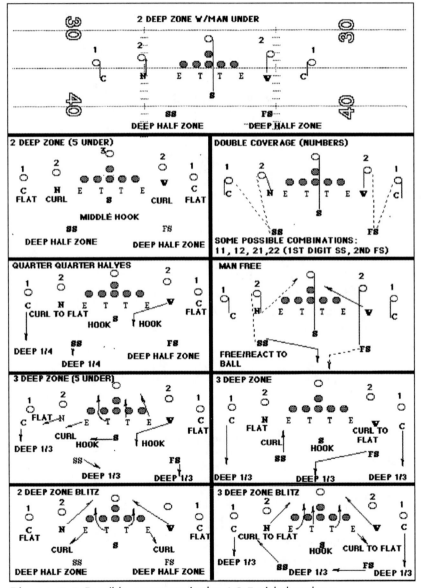

Diagram 5-4. Possible coverages in the 4-2-5 nickel package

Man-for-Man Coverage in the 4-2-5 Nickel

Man coverage can be broken down into three categories: man coverage with a free safety (cover 1/free), man coverage without a safety (used with blitzes), and man coverage with two-deep safeties (cover 2 man). In each of the man coverages without safety help, the safety is usually the adjuster, which means he covers for the blitzing defender. Also the corners can play either press-man coverage, or play off-man technique if desired. Diagrams 5-5 to 5-7 illustrate the three types of man coverage. Diagram 5-8 illustrates an example of zone coverage in this defensive package.

❑ *4-2-5 Switch Cover 1 Free Coverage*

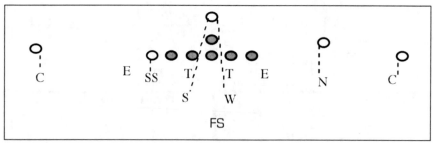

Diagram 5-5. 4-2-5 switch cover 1 free

Situational uses:

- When man coverage with a free safety is desirable
- Against a team that swings the back
- Against a team that runs screen to the remaining back
- Against a team that runs a draw

Strengths:

- Difficult for the tight end to get a free release off the ball
- The defensive back is covering the slot receiver.
- The free safety is in coverage.
- The remaining back is bracketed by two linebackers.
- Four-man rush
- The linebackers are facing the backfield for a screen or draw.

Weaknesses:

- Quick slants to side of swinging back
- Picks and rubs by twin receivers

❑ *Nickel Switch Cover 2 Man Coverage*

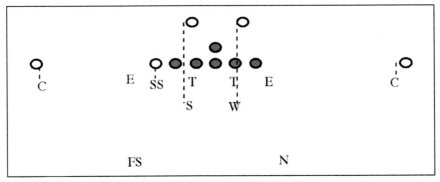

Diagram 5-6. Nickel switch cover 2 man

Nickel switch cover 2 man is a combination coverage with a two-deep zone, and man-for-man underneath. The free safety and nickel are responsible for the deep halves, while the corners are in press-man technique on the #1 to their respective sides. The strong safety is on the line of scrimmage, playing press technique on the tight end from an inside shade, denying him a clean release off the ball. The inside linebackers are playing man coverage on the remaining backs. The defensive end to the tight-end side aligns one yard outside the tight end and is angled in. The defensive tackles should be shaded strong on the offensive guards, with the weakside defensive end in an outside shade on the offensive tackle. The linebackers should be head-up on their respective backs, approximately five yards from the line of scrimmage.

Situational uses:

- Against an offense that lines up with a tight end on passing downs
- Against an offense that normally uses the running backs in pass protection
- Against flood routes

Strengths:

- The tight end and the wideouts are denied free release of the ball
- Four-man rush
- Two defenders are playing deep halves.
- Strong versus flood routes

Weaknesses:

- The linebackers are in man-for-man on the backs.
- Crossing routes underneath
- Picks and rubs
- Runs off tackle weak

❏ *4-2-5 Nickel Cover 1 Double Coverage*

A nickel defense should have the ability to negate the ability of the offense's best receiver by double-covering him on every play, making it as difficult as possible for him to get open. As a result, the offense may be forced either to throw into double-coverage or throw to someone other than their best. When an offensive coordinator recognizes double-coverage, one of the first things he will do to get him single-coverage is to line him up at various spots in the offensive formation. He may line up wide as a single receiver, he may line up in trips at any of the three spots, or he may be a tight end or in a slot. One defensive response to such an offensive move would be to call a "check-with-me" defense, and call the defensive double coverage on the line of scrimmage as soon as the alignment of the receiver is recognized. The defensive huddle call would be "nickel, cover 1 double ##," with the jersey number of the receiver to be doubled included in the call. The free safety plays bracket coverage on the receiver identified in the huddle, with the defender aligned over the identified receiver. For example, if an opponent's best receiver wears jersey number 88, the huddle call would be: "nickel, cover 1 double #88." If the #88 receiver lines up as the #1 (or outside most) receiver on the defensive left, the left corner will play outside press-man technique, while the free safety will play bracket technique with the corner, creating the double-coverage. Diagram 5-7 illustrates several examples of "nickel, cover 1 double #88."

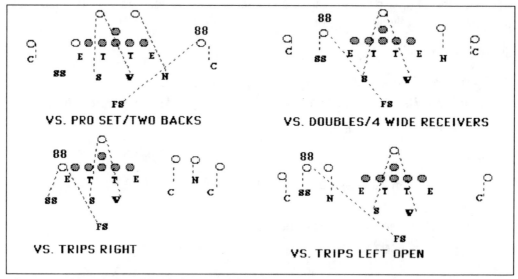

Diagram 5-7. Examples of "nickel, cover 1 double #88"

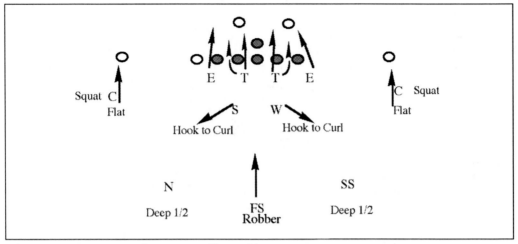

Diagram 5-8. 4-2-5 two-deep zone with a robber

Situational uses:

- Against a team that uses the drag, dig, post combination
- Against a team that runs deep crossing routes

Strengths:

- Four-man rush
- Strong versus drag, dig, post combination
- Strong versus deep crossing routes

Weakness:

- Flood routes

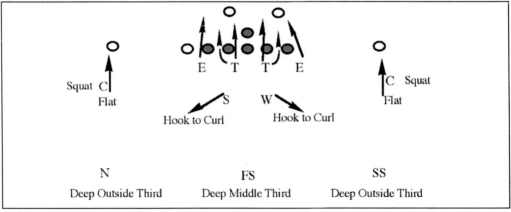

Diagram 5-9. Traditional three-deep zone

4-2-5 Nickel Blitzes

❏ *Nickel Sting Blitz*

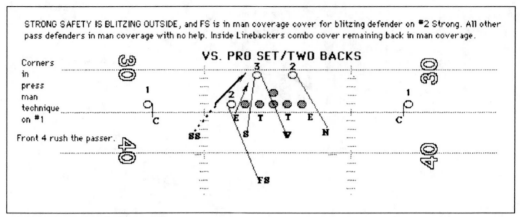

STRONG SAFETY IS BLITZING OUTSIDE, and FS is in man coverage cover for blitzing defender on #2 Strong. All other pass defenders in man coverage with no help. Inside Linebackers combo cover remaining back in man coverage.

VS. PRO SET/TWO BACKS

Corners in press man technique on #1

Front 4 rush the passer.

Diagram 5-10. Nickel sting blitz

Situational uses:

- Against a team that likes to roll out to the field
- Against a team that utilizes play-action to the strongside of the formation
- Against a team that utilizes a five- or seven-step drop by the quarterback
- Against a team that does not execute the hot route to the tight end with any consistency
- Against a team that does not throw the fade well

Strengths:

- Five-man rush
- The quarterback should have to get rid of the ball quickly.
- Strong versus play-action
- Strong versus roll out to the strongside of the formation

Weaknesses:

- No safety help for the corners or nickel back
- The hot route to the tight end is difficult to cover unless the free safety is aligned five- to seven-yards deep at the snap.

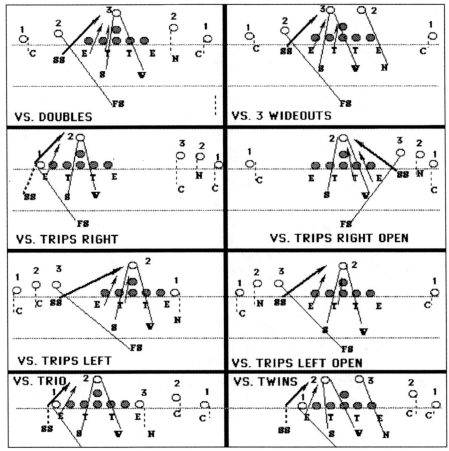

VS. DOUBLES

VS. 3 WIDEOUTS

VS. TRIPS RIGHT

VS. TRIPS RIGHT OPEN

VS. TRIPS LEFT

VS. TRIPS LEFT OPEN

VS. TRIO

VS. TWINS

Diagram 5-11. Nickel sting blitz versus various offensive formations

❑ *Nickel Strike Blitz*

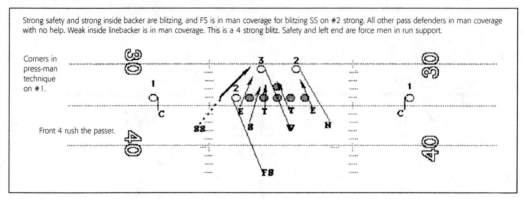

Diagram 5-12. Nickel strike blitz

Situational uses:

- Against one-back passing formations with slide protection
- Against a team that likes to roll out to the field
- Against a team that utilizes play-action to the strongside of the formation
- Against a team that utilizes a five- or seven-step drop by the quarterback
- Against a team that doesn't execute the hot route to the tight end with any consistency
- Against a team that doesn't throw the fade well

Strengths:

- Four-man overload to the strongside of the formation
- Six-man rush
- The quarterback should have to get rid of the ball quickly.
- Strong versus play-action
- Strong versus a roll-out to the strongside of the formation

Weaknesses:

- No safety help for the corners or nickel back
- The hot route to the tight end is difficult to cover unless the free safety is aligned five- to seven-yards deep at the snap.

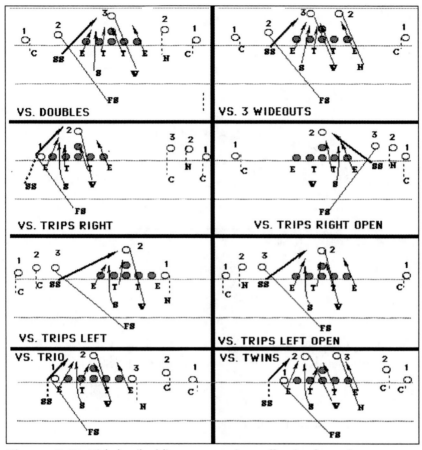

Diagram 5-13. Nickel strike blitz versus various offensive formations

❑ *4-2-5 Nickel Win Blitz*

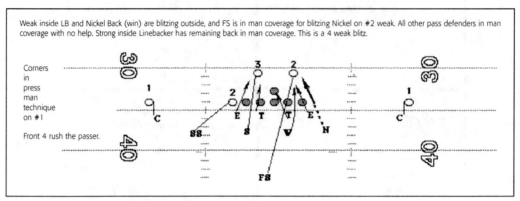

Diagram 5-14. 4-2-5 nickel win blitz

Situational uses:

- Against a team that likes to bootleg
- Against a team that utilizes play-action to the weakside of the formation
- Against a team that utilizes a five- or seven-step drop by the quarterback
- Against a team that does not protect well on their weakside

Strengths:

- Four-man overload to weakside of the formation
- Six-man rush
- The quarterback should have to get rid of the ball quickly.
- Strong versus bootleg
- Strong versus a roll-out to the weakside of the formation

Weaknesses:

- No safety help for the corners or nickel back
- The tight end drag is difficult to cover unless the middle linebacker walls him off.

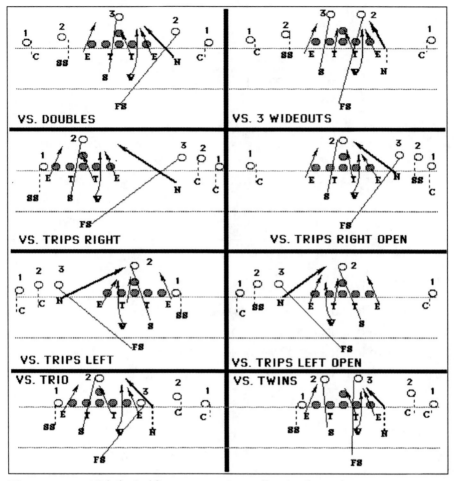

VS. DOUBLES

VS. 3 WIDEOUTS

VS. TRIPS RIGHT

VS. TRIPS RIGHT OPEN

VS. TRIPS LEFT

VS. TRIPS LEFT OPEN

VS. TRIO

VS. TWINS

Diagram 5-15. Nickel win blitz versus various offensive formations

❑ *Nickel Tom Plug Blitz*

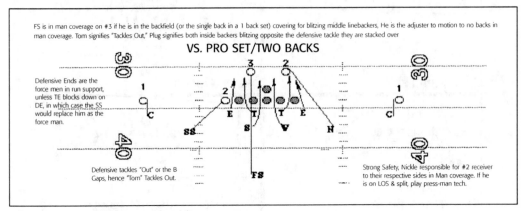

FS is in man coverage on #3 if he is in the backfield (or the single back in a 1 back set) covering for blitzing middle linebackers. He is the adjuster to motion to no backs in man coverage. Tom signifies "Tackles Out," Plug signifies both inside backers blitzing opposite the defensive tackle they are stacked over

VS. PRO SET/TWO BACKS

Defensive Ends are the force men in run support, unless TE blocks down on DE, in which case the SS would replace him as the force man.

Defensive tackles "Out" or the B Gaps, hence "Tom" Tackles Out.

Strong Safety, Nickle responsible for #2 receiver to their respective sides in Man coverage. If he is on LOS & split, play press-man tech.

Diagram 5-16. Nickel tom plug blitz

Situational uses:

- Against a team that uses one-back passing formations
- Against a team that utilizes play-action
- Against a team that utilizes a five- or seven-step drop by the quarterback
- Against a team that does not protect well up the middle

Strengths:

- Six-man rush
- The quarterback should have to get rid of the ball quickly.
- Strong versus play-action

Weaknesses:

- No safety help for the corners or nickel back
- The tight end drag is difficult to cover unless the middle linebacker walls him off.
- The free safety may have difficulty covering a swing pass to the back.
- The hot route by the tight end is difficult to cover unless the strong safety is aligned head-up on the tight end at five- to seven-yards at the snap.

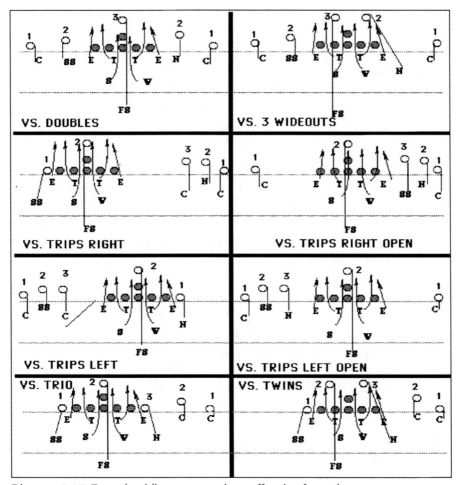

VS. DOUBLES

VS. 3 WIDEOUTS

VS. TRIPS RIGHT

VS. TRIPS RIGHT OPEN

VS. TRIPS LEFT

VS. TRIPS LEFT OPEN

VS. TRIO

VS. TWINS

Diagram 5-17. Tom plug blitz versus various offensive formations

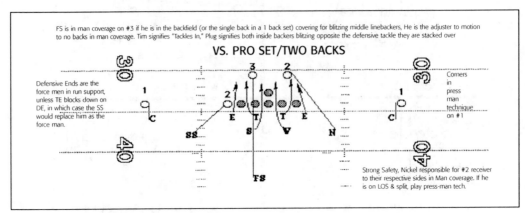

Diagram 5-18. 4-2-5 nickel tim plug blitz

Situational uses:

- Against a team that uses one-back passing formations
- Against a team that utilizes play-action
- Against a team that utilizes a five- or seven-step drop by the quarterback
- Against a team that does not protect well up the middle

Strengths:

- Six-man rush
- The quarterback should have to get rid of the ball quickly.
- Strong versus play-action
- Strong versus a roll-out to the weakside of the formation

Weaknesses:

- No safety help for the corners or nickel back
- The tight end drag is difficult to cover unless the middle linebacker walls him off.
- The free safety may have difficulty covering a swing pass to the back.
- The hot route by the tight end is difficult to cover unless the strong safety is aligned head-up on the tight end at five to seven yards at the snap.

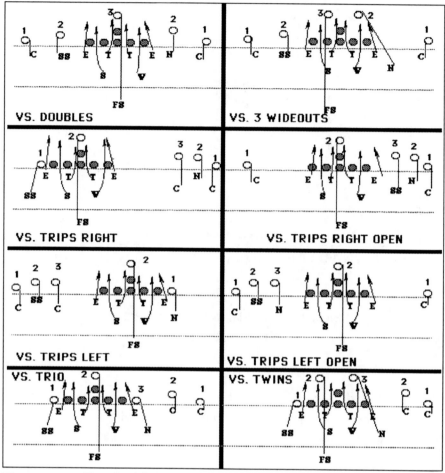

Diagram 5-19. Tim plug blitz versus various offensive formations

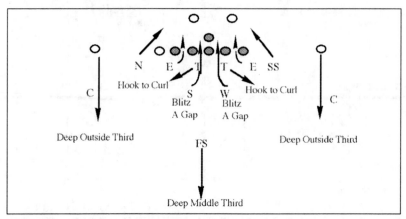

Diagram 5-20. 4-2-5 three-deep zone blitz

Situational uses:

- As a change-up to a conventional blitz with man coverage
- Against a team that runs predictable hot routes

Strengths:

- The quarterback does not know who is blitzing and who is dropping into coverage.
- The quarterback must make an accurate post-snap read.
- Defenders are dropped into normal hot-route areas.

Weaknesses:

- Flat coverage

❏ 4-2-5 Two-Deep Zone Blitz

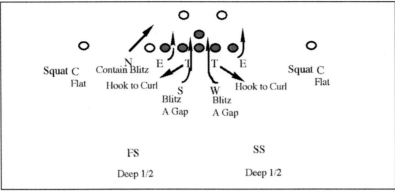

Diagram 5-21. Two-deep zone blitz

Situational uses:

- As a change-up to a conventional blitz with man coverage
- Against a team that runs predictable hot routes

Strengths:

- Strong flat coverage versus hot routes
- The quarterback does not know who is blitzing and who is dropping into coverage.
- The quarterback must make an accurate post-snap read.
- Defenders are dropped into normal hot-route areas.

Weaknesses:

- Middle hook zone

❑ *4-2-5 Three-Deep Zone Blitz*

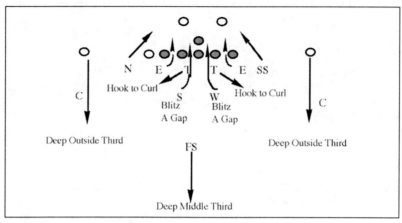

Diagram 5-22. 4-2-5 three-deep zone blitz

Situational uses:

- As a change-up to a conventional blitz with man coverage
- Against a team that runs predictable hot routes

Strengths:

- The quarterback does not know who is blitzing and who is dropping into coverage.
- The quarterback must make an accurate post-snap read.
- Defenders are dropped into normal hot-route areas.

Weaknesses:

- Flat coverage

Three-Deep Zones in the 4-2-5 Nickel

At least two ways exist to play a three-deep zone in the 4-2-5 nickel—both are illustrated in Diagrams 5-22 and 5-23. Diagram 5-22 shows a traditional three-deep zone with four pass rushers, four defenders playing short zones, and three defenders playing deep thirds. The second diagram (Diagram 5-23) shows a three-deep scheme with two squat corners. Utilizing both ways to play three-deep zone allows the defense to give different looks to the offense and keep the offense guessing as to which scheme the defense will use.

❑ *Traditional 4-2-5 Three-Deep, Four-Underneath Zone*

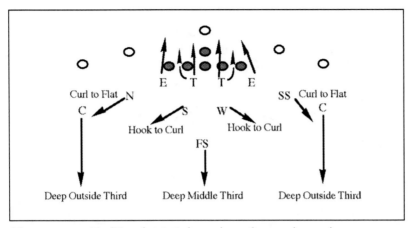

Diagram 5-23. Traditional 4-2-5 three-deep, four-underneath zone

Situational uses:

- When a three-deep, four-underneath coverage is preferable
- Against a team that throws to the flats
- Against a team that throws deep
- Against a team that may run wide in passing situations

Strengths:

- Five defensive backs in pass coverage
- Four-man rush
- Versus the tight end with two backs, eight defenders to play the run

Weaknesses:

- Three-level flood routes to the strongside or weakside
- Drag, post, dig combination

❏ *4-2-5 Three-Deep Zone With Squat Corners*

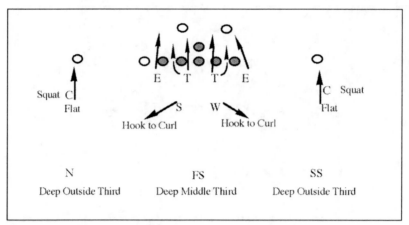

Diagram 5-24. 4-2-5 three-deep zone with squat corners

Situational uses:

- Against a team that uses two backs in passing situations
- When jamming the outside receivers off the line is preferable
- Against a team that uses the quick passing game
- Against a team that throws deep to the outside receivers
- As a prevent defense

Strengths:

- Prevents a free release off the ball by the outside receivers
- Four-man rush
- Three-deep zone
- Five defensive backs in pass coverage

Weaknesses:

- Difficult to play effectively versus twins, trips, or doubles

❑ *4-2-5 Quarter-Quarter-Half*

Quarter-quarter-half coverage is a hybrid pass coverage with elements of a three-deep zone and a two-deep zone. Basically, it is a two-deep zone to the weakside of a passing formation, and a three-deep zone to the strongside of the passing formation.

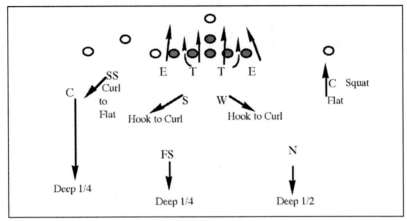

Diagram 5-25. 4-2-5 quarter-quarter-half

Situational uses:

- Against trips formations
- Against teams that throw flood routes
- Against a team that places the passing strength of the formation to the field
- Against a team that runs wide to the field

Strengths:

- Strong versus flood routes
- Four-man rush
- Free safety in deep quarter coverage can get to deep routes to the trips side faster than in the three-deep zone.

Weaknesses:

- Two short defenders on weakside of passing formation

The 3-3-5 Nickel Versus the Spread Offense

Personnel in the 3-3-5 Nickel

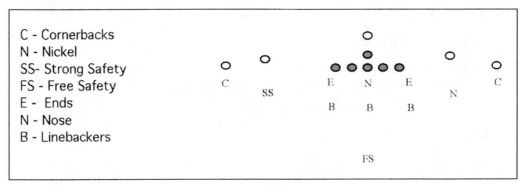

C - Cornerbacks
N - Nickel
SS- Strong Safety
FS - Free Safety
E - Ends
N - Nose
B - Linebackers

Diagram 6-1. Personnel employed in the 3-3-5 nickel

Situational uses:

- Utilized when a defense has better linebackers than pass rushers
- When dropping eight defenders into pass coverage is desirable
- Against teams who run wide
- Against a team that utilizes a three- or four-receiver formation
- Against a team that runs balanced passing formations
- Against a team that motions a back to the weakside of a formation

Strengths:

- Ability to play zone coverage with five defensive backs and three linebackers

- Strong flat coverage in two-deep or three-deep zone coverage
- Strong outside run support to either side of the formation
- Ability to match speed for speed in a three- or four-receiver set
- Ability to play man coverage with the free safety
- Ability to double-cover one or two receivers in man coverage
- Ability to bring four or five from either side of the formation
- Ability to zone blitz

Weaknesses:

- Three-man push rush unless blitzing
- Three-level flood routes are difficult to defend.
- Six-man front is easier to block than seven-man front on run plays.

Basic Premise of the 3-3-5 Nickel

The 3-3-5 nickel is characterized by using three down linemen in an odd front, three linebackers, and five defensive backs. The fifth defensive back will replace either a down lineman or linebacker. If a college 4-3 is the base defense, the fifth defensive back will replace one of the down linemen. If a 5-2 is the base defense, the fifth defensive back will replace one of the five down linemen, and another linebacker will replace the second down lineman. If a 3-4 is the base defense, the fifth defensive back replaces a linebacker.

Diagram 6-2 shows the base alignment and technique for each defender in the 3-3-5 nickel, as well as the basic responsibilities for run towards the defender, run away, key, and responsibility for drop-back pass. Keep in mind when reading the chart that many possible alignments are possible for the down linemen and linebackers.

The alignment listed in the chart for the left and right defensive ends is the outside eye of the offensive tackle. The technique that the ends should employ is noted as a squeeze technique, similar to the gap-control technique used in a 50 defense, which occurs in some situations, because the nickel package will see run, and the defensive ends will have to react accordingly. It is possible to abandon the squeeze technique and adopt a more aggressive pass-rush technique. The defensive ends are responsible for contain rush, unless they are stunting. If backfield run flow is towards them, they are responsible for the off-tackle gap. If flow is away from them, they are responsible for the quarterback bootleg or reverse.

The alignment for the nose is listed as head-up on the center. This recommendation is only meant as one possible alignment. Because shaded alignments are possible, the exact alignment of the nose should be made according to what is best for that particular defensive call. On any run play, the nose can play two gaps if he is aligned head-up, or if he aligns on a shade, he is responsible for the gap to that side. On flow away, the nose is responsible for pursuit and cutback. On a drop-back pass, he rushes the passer, either with a pre-determined pass-rush move or a stunt called in the huddle.

The precise alignment of the linebackers, "Stud," "Mike," and "Wild," is flexible. The Mike's base alignment should be head-up over the center or slightly shaded to either side. He should be at a depth of three-to-five yards, depending on down-and-distance. The outside linebackers, Stud and Wild in a base alignment, should be aligned on the outside shade of the tackle, three-to-five yards deep. Their exact alignment may vary when a blitz call or a stunt call is made. The Stud and Wild technique is listed as "squeeze/hat read," meaning they read through the uncovered guards on their side through to the backfield. The Mike linebacker reads the triangle (guard, center, guard, and backfield combination). Some coaches prefer that the linebackers read backs. The important point is to be consistent.

On flow toward either the Stud or Wild, they are each responsible for defending the gap assigned to them. The gap assigned to each outside linebacker is opposite the gap assigned to the defensive end in front of them. Usually, the gap that the inside linebacker is responsible for is opposite the gap assigned the nose in front of him. So, if the defensive end to his side is aligned on the inside shade of the offensive tackle (in the B-gap), the linebacker will be responsible for the C-gap. If the defensive tackle in front of him is aligned on the outside shade, the inside linebacker will be responsible for the B-gap. If flow is away from the linebackers, they should not turn their shoulders, but shuffle up and in towards the line of scrimmage. They should maintain backside leverage, not overpursue, and be ready to play cutback.

The strong safety and nickel defensive backs are mirrors of each other. The strong safety aligns to the strongside of the formation, over #2. His depth will depend on the pass coverage called. In press-man coverage, he will be on the line of scrimmage. In zone, he will be off the line of scrimmage. The technique of the strong safety and nickel will depend on the defensive call. They will blitz, play man coverage, or play zone coverage. In zone coverage, the strong safety and nickel will key the unit end (the outer-most player on the line of scrimmage in a three-point stance, either a tight end or tackle) through to the near back. If they are playing man coverage, they will key the receiver lined up in front of them.

The corners align on the #1 receiver to their side, unless there are trips opposite their side, in which case they align over the inside-most receiver. They key the unit end through to the near back. If they are playing man coverage, they will key the receiver lined up in front of them.

The free safety's alignment should be between 10 and 12 yards off the line of scrimmage, splitting the distance between the two widest receivers in the offensive formation. In man free or zone, he should key the guard nearest him through to the quarterback.

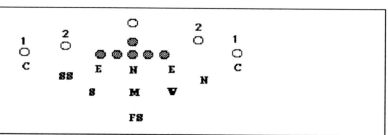

3-3-5 NICKEL FRONT & GAP RESPONSIBILITY CHART						
			BASIC RESPONSIBILITIES			
POSITION	ALIGN.	TECHNIQUE	RUN TO	RUN AWAY	KEY	DROPBACK PASS
LEFT END	OUTSIDE EYE OT	SQUEEZE 5 TECH.	C GAP IF M/M, FORCE	BOOTLEG REVERSE	BALL TO OT	CONTAIN RUSH OR STUNT
RIGHT END	OUTSIDE EYE OT	SQUEEZE 5 TECH	C GAP IF M/M, FORCE	BOOTLEG REVERSE	BALL TO OT	CONTAIN RUSH OR STUNT
NOSE	HEAD UP CENTER	2 GAP	A GAPS	CUTBACK PURSUIT	BALL TO G-C-G COMBO	TWO WAY GO UNLESS STUNT
STRONG OUTSIDE LB	STACK ON TACKLE	SQUEEZE HAT READ	B GAP	CUTBACK PURSUIT	STRONG GUARD	COVER CALL: MAN/ZONE BLITZ/COMBO
MIDDLE LB	STACK ON TACKLE	SQUEEZE HAT READ	A GAPS PURSUIT	CUTBACK PURSUIT BLOCKS	GUARDS' COMBO	COVER CALL: MAN/ZONE BLITZ/COMBO
WEAK OUTSIDE LB	STACK ON TACKLE	SQUEEZE HAT READ	B GAP	CUTBACK PURSUIT	WEAK GUARD	COVER CALL: MAN/ZONE BLITZ/COMBO
NICKEL	#2 STR OR OR TRIPS 3 WEAK	MAN/ZONE, BLITZ, OR DBL COVER	IF ZONE, FORCE	CUTBACK PURSUIT	ZONE-UNIT END TO #2; M/M-#2	COVER CALL: MAN/ZONE BLITZ/COMBO
STRONG SAFETY	2 STRONG OR TRIPS 3 WEAK	MAN/ZONE, BLITZ, OR DBL COVER	IF ZONE, FORCE	CUTBACK PURSUIT	ZONE-UNIT END TO #2; M/M-#2	COVER CALL: MAN/ZONE BLITZ/COMBO
WEAK CORNER	1 STRONG #2 ST TWINS #3 ST TRIPS	MAN/ZONE OR DOUBLE COVER	PITCH PASS LATE ON SUPPORT	PITCH PASS LATE ON SUPPORT	ZONE-UNIT END TO QB; MAN-REC	COVER CALL: MAN/ZONE OR DBL COVER
STRONG CORNER	1 STRONG #2 WK TWINS #3 WK TRIPS	MAN/ZONE OR DOUBLE COVER	PITCH PASS LATE ON SUPPORT	PITCH PASS LATE ON SUPPORT	ZONE-UNIT END TO QB MAN-REC	COVER CALL: MAN/ZONE OR DBL COVER
FREE SAFETY	PRE-SNAP 10-12 OFF LOS	MAN-FREE ZONE DBL COVER	INSIDE-OUT SUPPORT	CUTBACK PURSUIT	ONSIDE OG TO QB IN M/M, REC	COVER CALL: MAN/ZONE COVER FOR BLITZER

NOTE: THE ALIGNMENT OF THE DEFENSIVE BACKS ON ASSIGNED RECEIVERS DEPENDS ON THE COVER CALL.

Diagram 6-2. The 3-3-5 nickel front and gap responsibility chart

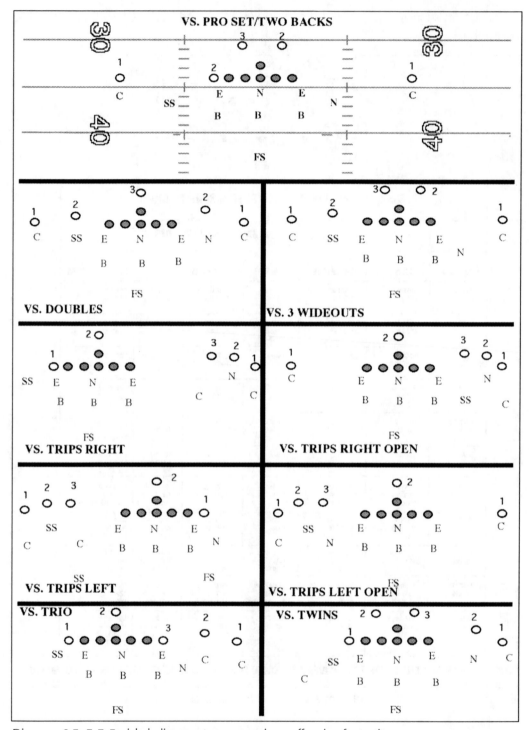

Diagram 6-3. 3-3-5 nickel alignment versus various offensive formations

Possible Coverages in the 3-3-5 Nickel

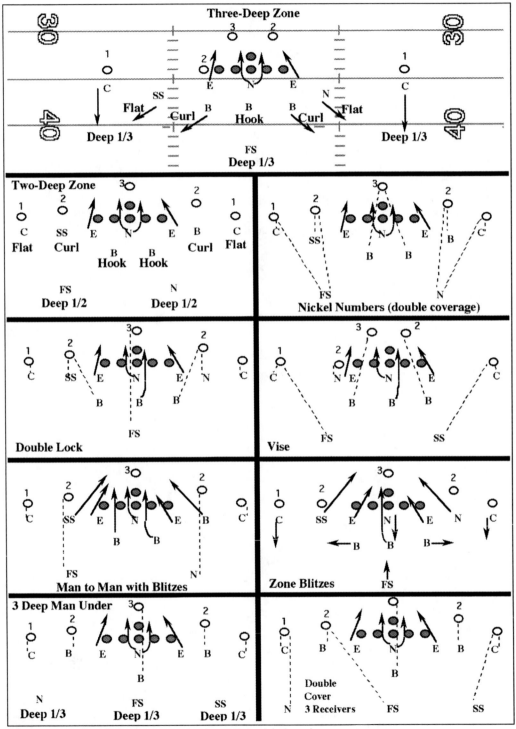

Diagram 6-4. Possible coverages in the 3-3-5 nickel package

❑ *3-3-5 Three-Deep Zone Coverage*

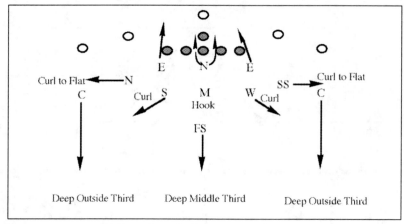

Diagram 6-5. 3-3-5 three-deep zone

Situational uses:

- Against teams that have strong pass protection
- Against teams that utilize a three-step drop

Strengths:

- Eight defenders dropping into zone coverage
- Five underneath zone defenders
- Three-deep zone defenders
- Strong versus outside run

Weaknesses:

- Three-man pass rush

❑ *3-3-5 Cover 3 Jam Coverage*

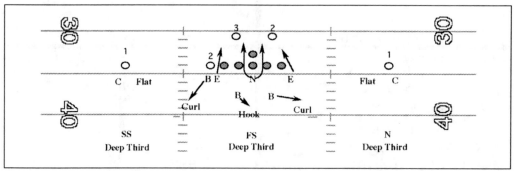

Diagram 6-6. 3-3-5 cover 3 jam

Situational uses:

- When three-deep zone is desirable with a jam on all receivers
- Against a team that aligns with a tight end in a passing situation
- Against a team that runs wide (good run force)
- Against a team that throws deep

Strengths:

- Eight defenders in pass coverage
- Jams all receivers off the ball
- Three-deep middle zones defended
- Strong versus outside running plays

Weaknesses:

- Three-man rush
- Void in the zone directly behind the linebackers and in front of the safeties
- Difficult to play versus one-back passing formations

❏ *3-3-5 Nickel Two-Deep Look Coverage*

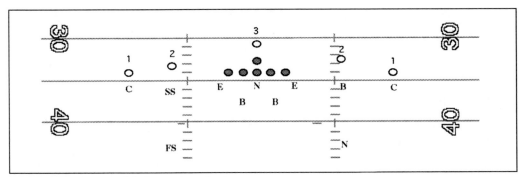

Diagram 6-7. 3-3-5 nickel two-deep look

Situational uses:

- When two safeties in deep coverage are preferred
- When double-coverage is preferred on at least one receiver
- When blitzing off a slot receiver
- Against one-back sets with slot receivers

Strengths:

- Two safeties are available to play in halves coverage.
- The ability to double-cover one or two receivers with safeties
- The possibility of bringing four to seven rushers easily
- Safeties cover for blitzing defenders
- Blitzes disguised easily

Weaknesses:

- There are five blockers to block five defenders on a run play.

❑ *3-3-5 Nickel Two-Deep Zone Coverage*

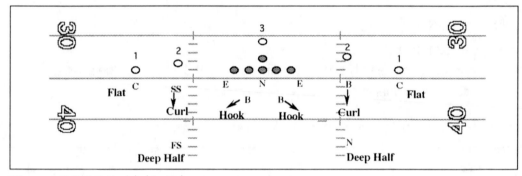

Diagram 6-8. 3-3-5 nickel two-deep zone

Situational uses:

- Against the quick passing game
- When two safeties in deep coverage are preferred
- Against a team that does not throw the ball downfield much
- Against a team that throws out routes both strong and weak
- When a jam on all receivers is desirable
- Against a team that runs wide

Strengths:

- Two safeties are available to play in halves coverage.
- The ability to jam all receivers off the line
- Eight defenders are in pass coverage.
- Six underneath zones are covered.

Weaknesses:

- Three-man rush

❑ *3-3-5 Nickel Numbers Coverage*

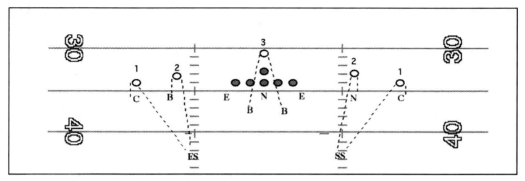

Diagram 6-9. 3-3-5 nickel numbers coverage

Situational uses:

- When double-coverage on one or two receivers is desirable

Strengths:

- The ability to double-cover one or two receivers
- The linebackers are bracketing the remaining back.
- Eight pass defenders are in coverage.
- The offense cannot use motion to isolate its receiver.

Weaknesses:

- No underneath help exists for single-coverage defenders on crossing or pick routes.
- Play-action pass
- There are five blockers to block five defenders on inside running plays.

Three Examples of Nickel Numbers Coverage

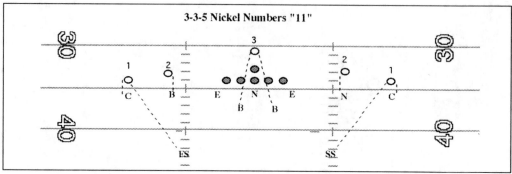

Diagram 6-10. 3-3-5 nickel numbers "11"

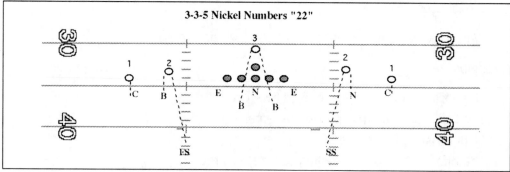

Diagram 6-11. 3-3-5 nickel numbers "22"

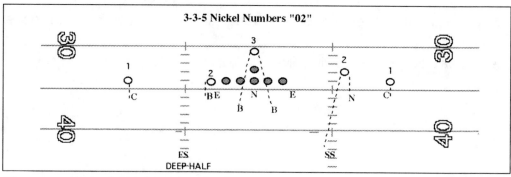

Diagram 6-12. 3-3-5 nickel numbers "02"

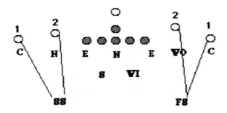

3-3-5 NICKEL NUMBERS FRONT & GAP RESPONSIBILITY CHART

POSITION	ALIGN.	TECHNIQUE	BASIC RESPONSIBILITIES			
			RUN TO	RUN AWAY	KEY	DROPBACK PASS
LEFT END	OUTSIDE EYE OT	SQUEEZE 5 TECH.	C GAP IF M/M, FORCE	BOOTLEG REVERSE	BALL TO OT	CONTAIN RUSH OR STUNT
NOSE	HEAD UP CENTER	2 GAP	A GAPS	CUTBACK PURSUIT	BALL TO G-C-G COMBO	TWO WAY GO UNLESS STUNT
RIGHT END	OUTSIDE EYE OT	SQUEEZE 5 TECH.	C GAP IF IF M/M, FORCE	BOOTLEG REVERSE	BALL TO OT	CONTAIN RUSH OR STUNT
STRONG INSIDE LB	STACK STRONG GUARD	SQUEEZE HAT READ	B GAP	CUTBACK PURSUIT	STRONG GUARD	COVER CALL: MAN/ZONE BLITZ/COMBO
WEAK INSIDE LB	STACK WEAK GUARD	SQUEEZE HAT READ	B GAP	CUTBACK PURSUIT	STRONG GUARD	COVER CALL: MAN/ZONE BLITZ/COMBO
WEAK OUTSIDE LB	#2 WEAK OR TRIPS 3 STRONG	MAN/ZONE, BLITZ, OR DBL COVER	IF ZONE, FORCE	CUTBACK PURSUIT	ZONE-UNIT END TO #2; M/M - #2	COVER CALL: MAN/ZONE BLITZ/COMBO
NICKEL	#2 STR OR TRIPS 3 WEAK	MAN/ZONE, BLITZ, OR DBL COVER	IF ZONE, FORCE	CUTBACK PURSUIT	ZONE-UNIT END TO #2; M/M - #2	COVER CALL: MAN/ZONE BLITZ/COMBO
FREE SAFETY	PRE-SNAP 10-12 OFF LOS	MAN-FREE ZONE DBL COVER	INSIDE-OUT SUPPORT	CUTBACK PURSUIT	RIGHT OG TO QB IN M/M, REC	COVER CALL: MAN/ZONE COVER FOR BLITZER
STRONG SAFETY	PRE-SNAP 10-12 OFF LOS	MAN-FREE ZONE DBL COVER	INSIDE-OUT SUPPORT	CUTBACK PURSUIT	LEFT OG TO QB IN M/M, REC	COVER CALL: MAN/ZONE COVER FOR BLITZER
WEAK CORNER	1 STRONG #2 ST TWINS #3 ST TRIPS	MAN/ZONE OR DOUBLE COVER	PITCH PASS LATE ON SUPPORT	PITCH PASS LATE ON SUPPORT	ZONE-UNIT END TO QB; MAN-REC	COVER CALL: MAN/ZONE OR DBL COVER
STRONG CORNER	1 STRONG #2 WK TWINS #3 WK TRIPS	MAN/ZONE OR DOUBLE COVER	PITCH PASS LATE ON SUPPORT	PITCH PASS LATE ON SUPPORT	ZONE-UNIT END TO QB; MAN-REC	COVER CALL: MAN/ZONE OR DBL COVER

NOTE: THE ALIGNMENT OF THE DEFENSIVE BACKS ON ASSIGNED RECEIVERS DEPENDS ON THE COVER CALL.

Diagram 6-13. The 3-3-5 nickel numbers front and gap responsibility chart

❏ *3-3-5 Vise Coverage*

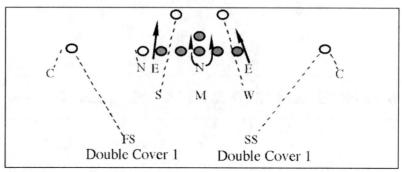

Diagram 6-14. 3-3-5 vise coverage

Situational uses:

- Against a two-back set when double-coverage on the wideouts is desired
- Against a team that rarely throws to the backs
- Against a team that rarely throws to the tight end

Strengths:

- Double-coverage on both wideouts
- Seven in the box versus run
- Strong versus flood routes
- Strong versus drag, dig, post combination

Weaknesses:

- Three-man rush
- Difficult for linebackers to cover swing routes by the backs
- Difficult for linebackers to cover backs who are aligned in the slots

❏ *3-3-5 Double-Lock Coverage*

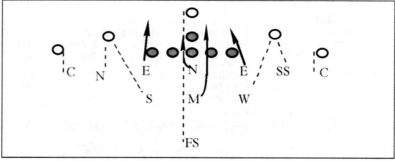

Diagram 6-15. 3-3-5 double-lock coverage

Situational uses:

- Against a team with talented receivers who are aligned in the slot
- Against a team that aligns with two receivers to each side of the offensive formation

Strengths:

- Four-man rush
- Double coverage on the slot receivers
- The free safety is deep in coverage if the back blocks.

Weaknesses:

- The free safety may have trouble getting to a swing pass to the back.
- No help exists for defenders who are covering wideouts.

❑ *3-3-5 Nickel Strike Coverage*

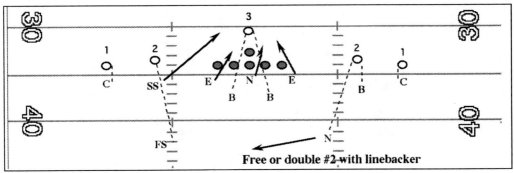

Diagram 6-16. 3-3-5 nickel strike coverage

Situational uses:

- Against teams that roll out to their right
- Against play-action
- Against a team that utilizes a five- or seven-step drop

Strengths:

- Five-man rush
- Strong versus a roll-out
- Strong versus a play-action pass
- Possible to double-cover receivers on the opposite side of the blitzing defensive back
- The safety covers for the blitzing defender.
- The blitz is disguised easily.

Weaknesses:

- A quick out by the slot receiver is difficult for the safety to cover.
- A swing pass to the remaining back who is away from the inside linebacker is difficult to cover.

❏ *3-3-5 Nickel Blitzes*

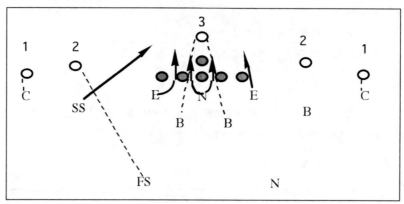

Diagram 6-17. 3-3-5 nickel storm blitz

Situational uses:

- Against teams that roll out to their right
- Against play-action
- Against a team that utilizes a five- or seven-step drop

Strengths:

- Four-man rush
- Strong versus a roll out
- Strong versus a play-action pass
- Possible to double-cover receivers on the opposite side of the blitzing defensive back
- The safety covers for the blitzing defender.
- The blitz is disguised easily.

Weaknesses:

- A quick out by the slot receiver is difficult for the safety to cover.

❑ *3-3-5 Nickel Twister Blitz*

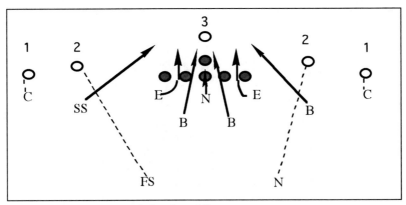

Diagram 6-18. 3-3-5 nickel twister blitz

Situational uses:

- Against teams that roll out to either side
- Against play-action
- Against a team that utilizes a five- or seven-step drop

Strengths:

- Seven-man rush forces the quarterback to get rid of the ball quickly.
- Strong versus a roll-out
- Strong versus a play-action pass
- Safeties can cover for the blitzing defender.
- The blitz is disguised easily.

Weaknesses:

- A quick out by the slot receiver is difficult for the safety to cover.
- A swing pass to the remaining back away from the inside linebacker is difficult to cover.
- The outside blitzer must use a blitz-peel technique in case the back swings.

□ *3-3-5 Cyclone Blitz*

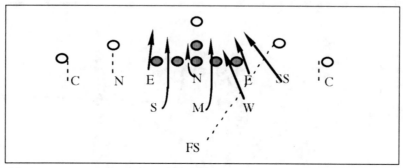

Diagram 6-19. 3-3-5 cyclone blitz

Situational uses:

- Against a team that rolls out to the defensive right
- Against a team that uses a five- or seven-step drop

Strengths:

- Seven-man rush versus six blockers in pass protection if a back is used
- The defensive backs are covering the slot receivers.

Weaknesses:

- The free safety may have trouble covering a quick out by the slot unless he is aligned head-up at five to seven yards at the snap.
- The strong safety and right end must blitz-peel if the back swings.
- No safety help exists for the man-to-man defenders.

□ *3-3-5 Slant Plug Blitz*

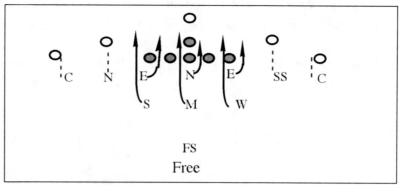

Diagram 6-20. 3-3-5 slant plug blitz

Situational uses:

- Against teams that use a single back in protection
- Against teams that use play-action
- Against teams that utilize a five- or seven-step drop

Strengths:

- Six-man rush
- The quarterback will have to get rid of the ball quickly.
- The defensive backs are covering the wideouts.
- The free safety is deep in coverage.

Weaknesses:

- The contain rushers (the stud linebacker and the left end) must blitz-peel for a swinging back.

❑ *3-3-5 Hurricane Blitz*

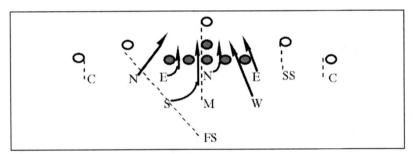

Diagram 6-21. 3-3-5 hurricane blitz

Situational uses:

- Against a team that rolls out
- Against a team that uses a five- or seven-step drop

Strengths:

- Seven-man rush
- The quarterback will have to get rid of the ball quickly.
- The defensive backs are covering the slot receivers.

Weaknesses:

- No safety help exists for the man defenders.
- The free safety may have trouble covering a quick out by the slot unless he is aligned five to seven yards head-up at the snap.

7

The Dime Package Versus the Spread Offense

Dime defenses originated as an extension of nickel defenses. A dime defense is characterized by six defensive backs (instead of five in the nickel) and is played with either an odd front (3-2) or even front (4-1). In an odd-front defense, the two defensive backs entering the game would replace the two outside linebackers in a 3-4 or the two defensive tackles in a 5-2 with five down linemen. In an even-front defense, the two incoming defensive backs would replace the two outside linebackers.

Dime defenses are schemes that are used to defend the pass in obvious passing situations, especially against four-wide receiver or empty backfield offensive formations. They are effective against the pass in part because the speed of the six defensive backs matches up better with the speed of the offense. The theory is that defensive backs play better in space than linebackers, and therefore, they are more effective defending the pass.

While the defense that uses a dime package may have great success defending the pass, the obvious disadvantage is that linemen and linebackers play the run more effectively. If an offense decides to run the ball versus a dime defense, they have a decided advantage.

The 4-1-6 dime is played with four down lineman, one middle linebacker, and six defensive backs. Usually, the defensive backs include two corners, two safeties, a nickel back, and a dime back. As a general rule the nickel and dime backs replace one linebacker and one down lineman. The 4-1-6 dime has a variety of coverages. These coverages can be classified as either man coverages, zone coverages, or combination coverages.

4-1-6 Dime Defense

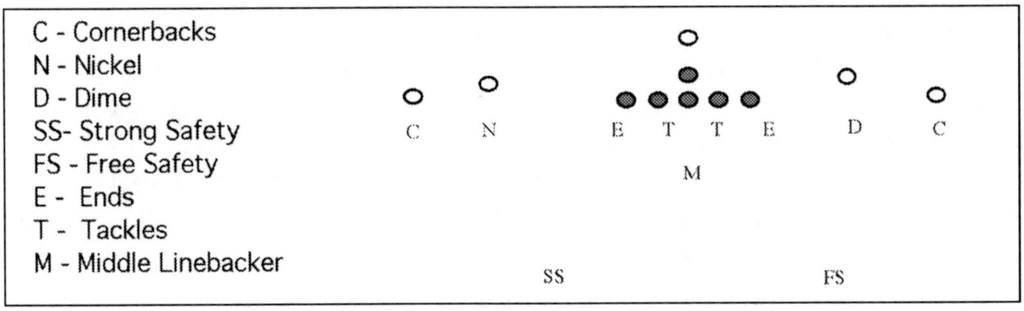

C - Cornerbacks
N - Nickel
D - Dime
SS - Strong Safety
FS - Free Safety
E - Ends
T - Tackles
M - Middle Linebacker

C   N   E   T   T   E   D   C

M

SS   FS

Diagram 7-1. 4-1-6 dime defense

Situational uses:

- Against an offense that throws the ball with four or five receivers most of the time
- On obvious passing downs
- To double-cover one or more receivers
- As a prevent defense to eliminate the big play

Strengths:

- Four-man rush
- Matches speed for speed by using two extra defensive backs
- Ability to double cover one or more of the receivers at any time
- Ability to blitz a linebacker or any of the six defensive backs with a free safety
- Ability to play robber coverage with a free safety
- Ability to play two-deep, three-deep, or four-deep coverage
- Ability to zone blitz

Weaknesses:

- Weak against the run if four-wide receiver formations are used
- The middle linebacker must cover a single back in man coverage.

Choosing a Type of Coverage

Man Coverage

Four reasons exist to use man coverage. First, man-to-man is preferred when the defense has superior personnel, and can line up and be successful dominating the offensive receivers. Second, press man coverage is employed when the defense is blitzing. As a result, an easy quick route, that is all the quarterback should have time to throw, is eliminated. Third, man coverage is used when teams are running flood patterns to beat zones, such as a multiple level pattern. Man coverage will allow the defense to match up and get better odds against these patterns. And fourth, man coverage is used to take away the short pass, such as hitches, quick outs, or slants. Man-to-man press coverages are designed both to disrupt the timing between the quarterback and the receivers and to put pressure on the quarterback's decision or read sequence. A great advantage exists to playing man coverage because it frees up the safeties to either play deep zone (in combination coverage) and guard against the deep pass, play strong run support, blitz, or cover for a blitzing defender.

Zone Coverage

Several reasons exist to use zone coverages. First, zone coverage can be used to keep the ball in front of the defense and eliminate the big play. Second, zone coverage can be employed if a team is playing against superior receivers, enabling the corners to jam them off the line and slow them down. Third, zone coverage can be used if a team is throwing short-to-medium timing routes, which allows defenders to jam the receivers off the line and disrupt their timing. Third, zone coverage can be employed when a team executes screens and draws. This coverage allows zone defenders to recognize these plays faster because they are facing the quarterback. And finally, a match-up zone can be used if a team has been successful running crossing routes or picks and rubs. Zone coverage will eliminate the effectiveness of their picks. Zone coverages are designed to take away the deep ball, as well as certain routes. For that reason, certain zones should be played to take away certain routes. To prevent the deep pass, a three-deep zone should be used. To take away the short, three-step game, a two-deep zone with squat corners should be employed. To take away flood routes to the field, quarters coverage should be played.

Combination Coverages

It is advantageous to get into combination coverages for a variety of reasons. To play man coverage with a safety net, play man under with either one or two safeties deep. Second, to stop crossing routes, which are effective against man coverage, play man or zone with a robber to take away those routes. Third, to ensure a receiver will run into a man defender no matter what his release, play a combo coverage. Fourth, combination coverage allows double coverage on one receiver, while playing man on the other receivers.

To beat the truly great passing offenses, it is beneficial to play man, zone, and combination coverage to answer any passing attack the offense may throw at the defense. The versatility of playing these various coverages will force significant preparation time for the quarterback. Furthermore, it will reduce his ability to make sound, consistent post-snap reads in order to have a chance to be effective.

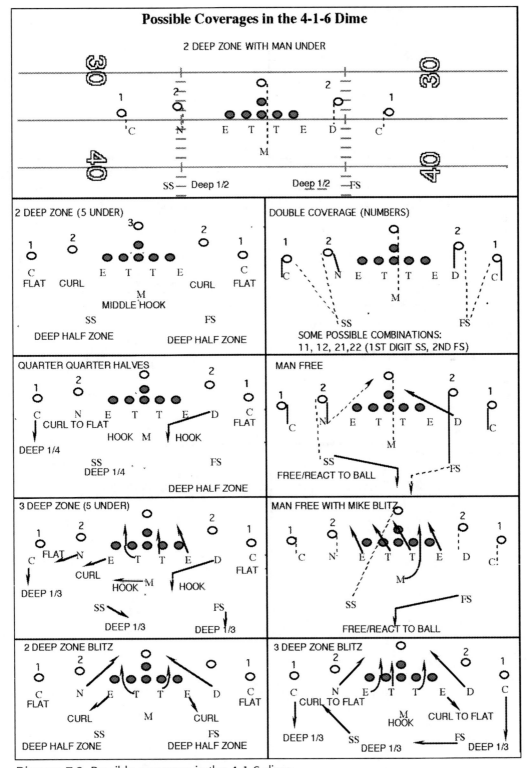

Diagram 7-2. Possible coverages in the 4-1-6 dime

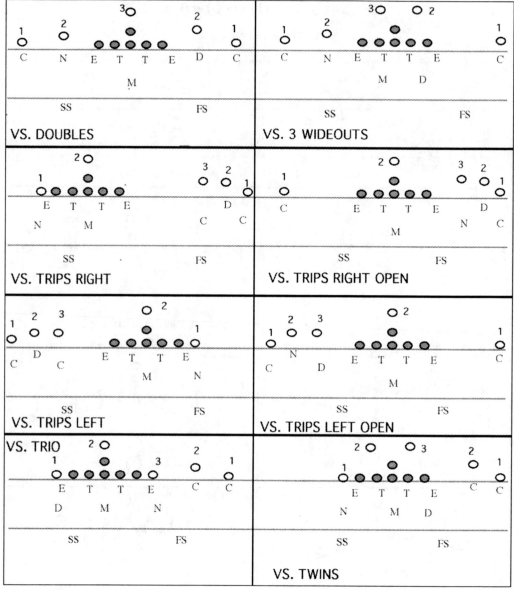

Diagram 7-3. 4-1-6 dime alignment versus various offensive formations

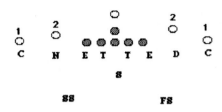

4-1-6 DIME FRONT & GAP RESPONSIBILITY CHART

POSITION	ALIGN.	TECHNIQUE	BASIC RESPONSIBILITIES			
			RUN TO	RUN AWAY	KEY	DROPBACK PASS
LEFT END	OUTSIDE EYE OT	SQUEEZE 5 TECH.	OFF TACKLE; IF M/M FORCE	BOOTLEG REVERSE	BALL TO OT	CONTAIN RUSH OR STUNT
RIGHT END	OUTSIDE EYE OT	SQUEEZE 5 TECH.	OFF TACKLE; IF M/M, FORCE	BOOTLEG REVERSE	BALL TO OT	CONTAIN RUSH OR STUNT
LEFT TACKLE	SOLID OFFENSIVE GUARD	RUSH 2	TWO GAP INSIDE/OUT PLAYER	PURSUIT CUTBACK	BALL TO OG	TWO GAP DEPENDS ON STUNT/BLITZ
RIGHT TACKLE	SOLID OFFENSIVE GUARD	RUSH 2	TWO GAP INSIDE/OUT PLAYER	PURSUIT CUTBACK	BALL TO OG	TWO GAP DEPENDS ON STUNT/BLITZ
STUD ILB	B GAP STRONG OR STACK	SQUEEZE HAT READ	OPPOSITE GAP OF DT IN FRONT	CUTBACK PURSUIT	OG CALL	COVER CALL: MAN/ZONE BLITZ/COMBO
NICKEL	2 STRONG OR TRIPS 3 WEAK	MAN/ZONE, BLITZ, OR DBL COVER	IF ZONE, FORCE	CUTBACK PURSUIT	ZONE-UNIT END TO #2; M/M - #2	COVER CALL: MAN/ZONE BLITZ/COMBO
DIME	#2 WEAK OR TRIPS 3 STRONG	MAN/ZONE BLITZ, OR DBL COVER	IF ZONE, FORCE	CUTBACK PURSUIT	ZONE-UNIT END TO #2; M/M - #2	COVER CALL: MAN/ZONE BLITZ/COMBO
WEAK CORNER	1 STRONG #2 ST TWINS #3 ST TRIPS	MAN/ZONE OR DOUBLE COVER	PITCH PASS LATE ON SUPPORT	PITCH PASS LATE ON SUPPORT	ZONE-UNIT END TO QB; MAN-REC	COVER CALL: MAN/ZONE OR DBL COVER
STRONG CORNER	1 STRONG #2 WK TWINS #3 ST TRIPS	MAN/ZONE OR DOUBLE COVER	PITCH PASS LATE ON SUPPORT	PITCH PASS LATE ON SUPPORT	ZONE-UNIT END TO QB; MAN-REC	COVER CALL: MAN/ZONE OR DBL COVER
FREE SAFETY	PRE-SNAP 10-12 OFF LOS	MAN-FREE ZONE DBL COVER	INSIDE-OUT SUPPORT	CUTBACK PURSUIT	RIGHT OG TO QB IN M/M, REC	COVER CALL: MAN/ZONE COVER FOR BLITZER
STRONG SAFETY	PRE-SNAP 10-12 OFF LOS	MAN-FREE ZONE DBL COVER	INSIDE-OUT SUPPORT	CUTBACK PURSUIT	LEFT OG TO QB IN M/M, REC	COVER CALL: MAN/ZONE COVER FOR BLITZER

NOTE: THE ALIGNMENT OF THE DEFENSIVE BACKS ON ASSIGNED RECEIVERS DEPENDS ON THE COVER CALL. THE GAP ASSIGNMENT OF THE INSIDE BACKERS AND DEFENSIVE TACKLES IS FLEXIBLE.

Diagram 7-4. 4-1-6 dime front and gap responsibility chart

Double-Coverage Using the Numbers System

The "numbers" system of double-coverage enables a dime defense to double cover one or more of the offense's receivers using a simple numbering system. In this system, eligible receivers are assigned a number (1 through 3) based on their offensive alignment (Diagram 7-5).

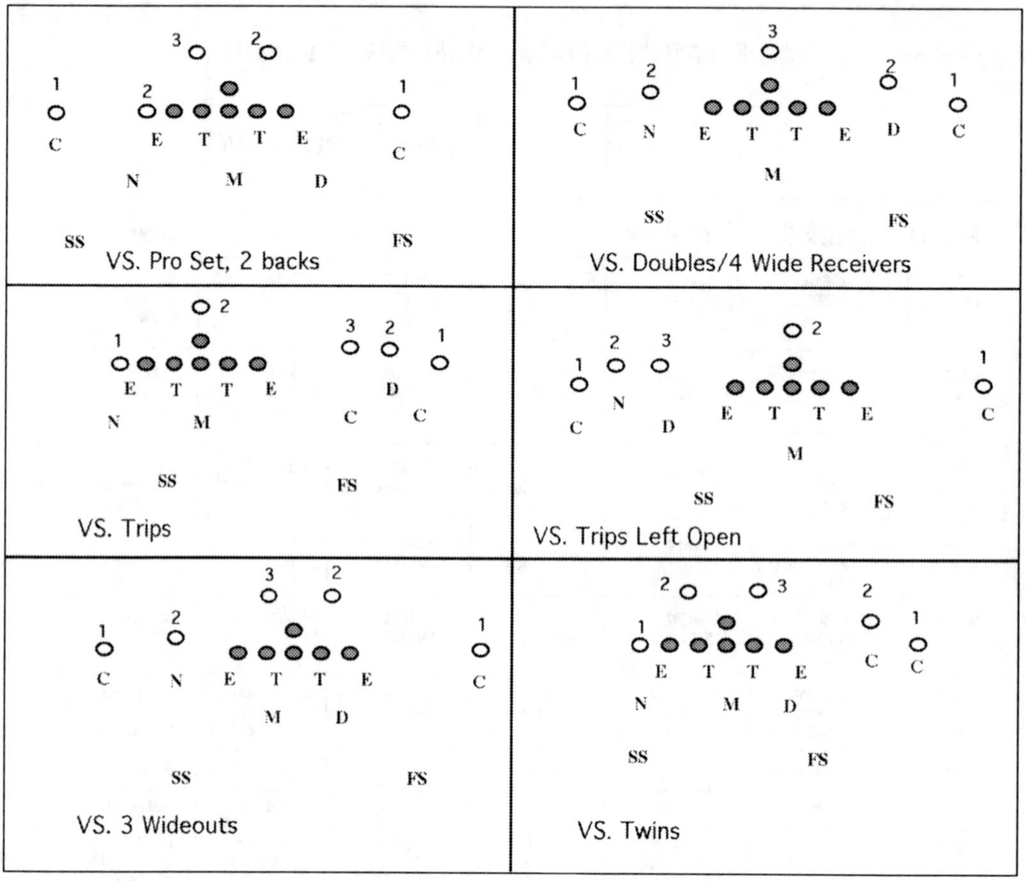

VS. Pro Set, 2 backs	VS. Doubles/4 Wide Receivers
VS. Trips	VS. Trips Left Open
VS. 3 Wideouts	VS. Twins

Diagram 7-5. Numbering the receivers

It should be noted that the numbers begin with the number one on each side, starting on the outside and working their way inside. Whatever alignment the offense chooses to utilize, the receivers are numbered according to their alignment. Once the defenders understand the numbers system, the huddle call should be taught next. For example, the huddle call might be "DIME NUMBERS 01."

- Part one of the call, "dime," signifies the front with dime personnel.
- Part two of the call, "numbers," signifies to the middle linebacker and defensive backs that man-to-man double coverage is called.

- Part three of the call, "01," identifies which receiver(s) is to be double-covered. The first digit, 0, applies to the safety aligned on the defensive LEFT side of the defensive formation. The second digit, 1, applies to the safety aligned on the defensive RIGHT side of the formation. For example:

Left Safety call: "Dime Numbers ##"

First digit	Coverage responsibility:
0	The left safety covers the deep-half zone.
1	The left safety brackets the first receiver on the left side.
2	The left safety brackets the second receiver on the left side.
3	The left safety brackets the third receiver on the left side.

Right Safety call: "Dime Numbers ##"

Second digit	Coverage responsibility:
0	The right safety covers the deep-half zone.
1	The right safety brackets the first receiver on the right side.
2	The right safety brackets the second receiver on the right side.
3	The right safety brackets the third receiver on the right side.

Therefore, if the huddle call was, "Dime Numbers 11," each safety would bracket the first, or outer-most, receiver to his respective side (Diagram 7-6).

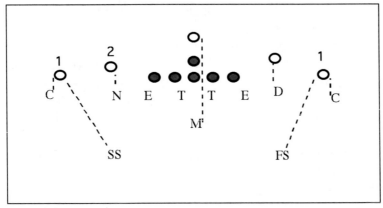

Diagram 7-6. Dime numbers 11

If the huddle call was, "Dime Numbers 21," the left safety would bracket the second receiver inside, and the right safety would bracket the number 1 receiver to his side (Diagram 7-7). It should be noted that any combination of receivers may be double-covered using the numbers system.

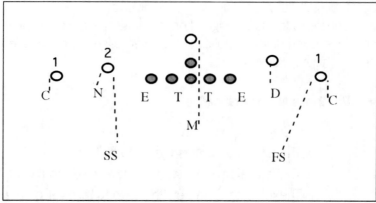

Diagram 7-7. Dime numbers 21

Dime Numbers, Check-With-Me

Any nickel or dime defense should have the ability to negate the ability of the offense's best receiver by double-covering him on every play, thereby making it as difficult as possible for him to get open. In this way, the offense may be forced either to throw into double-coverage, or throw to someone other than their best receiver. When an offensive coordinator recognizes double-coverage, one of the first things he will do to get single coverage is align the receiver at various spots in the offensive formation. He may line up wide as a single receiver; he may line up in trips at any of the three spots; he may be a tight end or a slot. One defensive answer to such an offensive move would be to call a "check-with-me" defense. Then, call the defensive double-coverage (numbers) on the line of scrimmage as soon as the alignment of the receiver is recognized. The defensive huddle call would be "DIME NUMBERS, CHECK-WITH-ME." If the offense's best receiver lines up as the #1 (or outside most) receiver on the defensive left, the entire defensive secondary would start yelling (communicating) "CHECK 10, CHECK 10." This signal will lock-in the call for double-coverage on their best receiver, who is aligned on the defensive left as the outside-most receiver. The left corner and left safety would double-cover him, and nickel, dime, Mike linebacker, and right corner would play press man-to-man technique. The right safety would be playing a "0" technique, which is a deep 1/2 zone on the defensive right. Diagram 7-8 illustrates several examples of "DIME NUMBERS, CHECK-WITH-ME," using #87 as the offensive receiver to be double-covered.

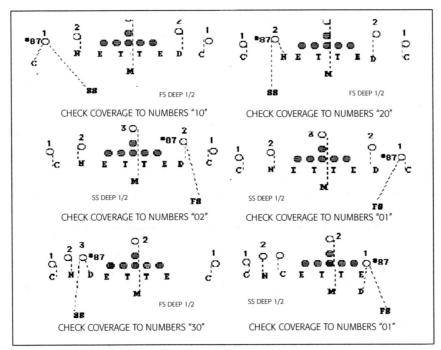

Diagram 7-8. Examples of "dime numbers, check-with-me"

Dime Numbers "00"

Dime numbers "00" is played with four down linemen, one middle linebacker, and six defensive backs. The middle linebacker is playing man coverage on the remaining back. The corners are playing either head-up or inside-press technique on the #1 receivers to their respective sides, while the nickel and dime are playing head-up or inside-press technique on the #2 receivers to their respective sides. In the case of three receivers (trips) to one side of the offensive formation, the corner would be responsible for #1, while the nickel and dime would be responsible for #2 and #3. The "00" call signifies that the safeties have no man coverage responsibility, and are playing deep-halves. Basically, this coverage is a two-deep, man-under combination (Diagram 7-9).

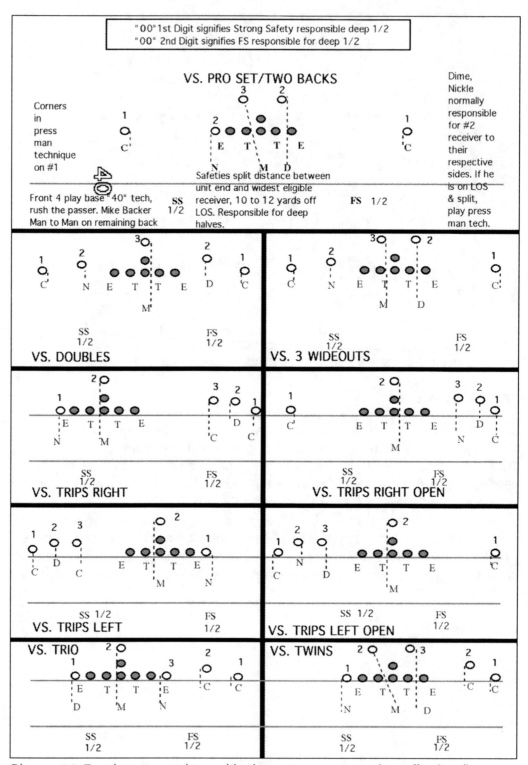

Diagram 7-9. Two-deep man-under combination coverage versus various offensive alignments

Situational uses:

- This coverage is good to play when man coverage is desirable with a safety net.

Strengths:

- Man-for-man underneath with deep help
- Four-man pass rush

Weaknesses:

- No underneath help for cover men on crossing routes or pick routes
- Play-action pass

Drills to teach the coverage:

- One-on-one drills with the quarterback, receiver, and defender; the defender plays press-man technique on the receiver.
- Hash drills for safeties; the safeties start on the hashes; the coach runs three verticals down the field, equidistant from one another; the safeties must stay on the hash until the ball is thrown.

Dime Numbers "11"

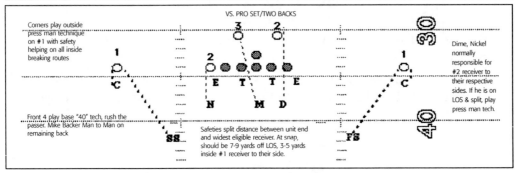

Diagram 7-10. Dime numbers 11

"Dime numbers 11" is played with four down linemen, one middle linebacker, and six defensive backs. The middle linebacker is playing man coverage on the remaining back. The corners are playing outside-press technique on the #1 receivers to their respective sides, while the nickel and dime are playing head-up or inside-press technique on the #2 receivers to their respective sides. In the case of the three receivers (trips) to one side of the offensive formation, the corner would be responsible for #1, while the nickel and dime are responsible for #2 and #3. The "11" call signifies that the safeties are bracketing the #1 receivers to their respective sides. This coverage is combination coverage—basically, double-coverage on the outside receivers with press-man coverage on the other three eligibles.

Situational uses:

- This coverage is good for taking away the outside receivers with double-coverage on each.
- This coverage is excellent against teams that throw quick-out routes, deep-comeback routes, and post-corner routes.
- Because of the outside leverage by the corners, this coverage is excellent to run when teams must get their receivers out of bounds to conserve the clock.

Strengths:

- Double-coverage on X and Z receivers
- Safety help on deep routes
- Strong versus flood routes
- Picks involving X and Z are less effective because they are double-covered.
- Four-man pass rush

Weaknesses:

- No help on crossing routes underneath
- No help on picks for linebackers, nickel, and dime
- The linebacker is man-for-man with a back.
- Vulnerable to swing passes when the other receivers run deep; the linebacker has no help.
- Secondary run support is limited because the defensive backs are in man coverage and may have their backs turned to the quarterback when in press coverage.

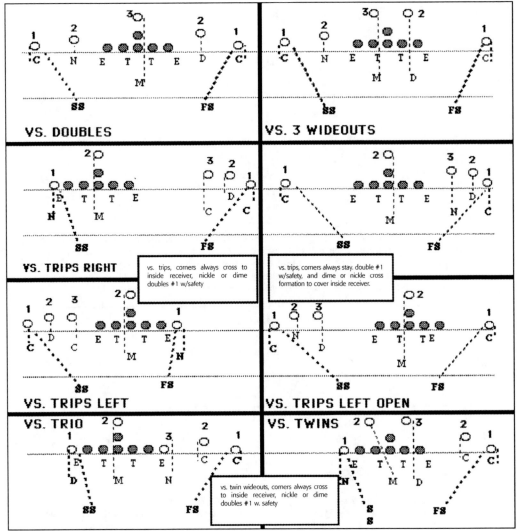

Diagram 7-11. Dime numbers "11" versus various offensive formations

Numbers "11" Pre-Snap Bracket Drill

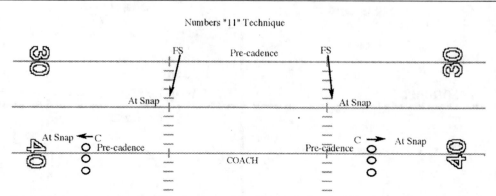

Step 1: Safeties and corner practice moving from a two-deep, man under look to bracket technique alignment used in numbers coverage. Pre-cadence, the safety is at 10-12 yards deep on the hash, and the corner is showing an inside press man technique alignment. Corner and Safety must practice timing their moves so that at the snap, the safety is at seven yards inside and 3-4 yards inside the outside receiver. The corner must time his step, so that at the snap, he is aligned with his inside eye to the receiver's ouside eye. Coach must use opponent's snap cadence if possible.

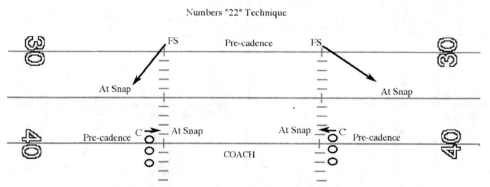

Step 1: Safeties and corner practice moving from a two-deep cover 2 look to bracket technique alignment used in numbers "22" coverage. Pre-cadence, the safety is at 10-12 yards deep on the hash, and the corner is showing outside squat technique alignment. Corner and Safety must practice timing their moves so that at the snap, the safety is at seven yards outside and 3-4 yards ouyside the inside receiver. The corner must time his step, so that at the snap, he is aligned with his outside eye to the receiver's inside eye. Coach must use opponent's snap cadence if possible.

Diagram 7-12. Numbers pre-snap bracket drill

Numbers "11" Bracket Drill

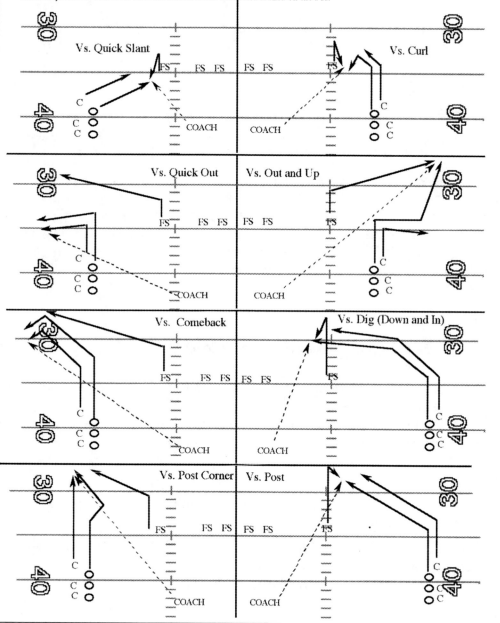

Numbers "11" Bracket Drill
Numbers "11" Technique

Safeties and corners practice bracket technique alignment used in numbers "11" coverage vs. various routes. At the snap, the safety is at seven yards inside and 3-4 yards inside the outside receiver. At the snap, the corner is aligned with his inside eye to the receiver's ouside eye, playing outside press man technique. After running the drill with one side of the secondary, run the drill with both safeties and man defenders locked on the #1s.

Diagram 7-13. Numbers "11" bracket drill

Dime Numbers "22"

"22" 1st digit signifies left (SS) doubling all routes to his side on #2 to left side of formation.*
"22" 2nd digit signifies right (FS) doubling all routes to his side on #2 to right side of formation.*

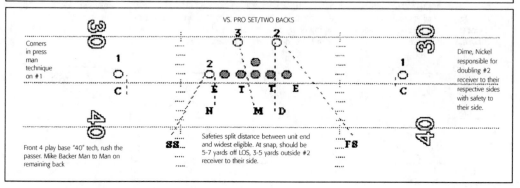

Diagram 7-14. Dime numbers "22"

"Dime numbers 22" is played with four down linemen, one middle linebacker, and six defensive backs. The middle linebacker is playing man coverage on the remaining back. The corners are playing head-up or inside-press technique on the #1 receivers to their respective sides. The "22" call signifies that the safeties are bracketing the #2 receivers to their respective sides. This coverage is combination coverage—basically, double-coverage on the #2 receivers with press-man coverage on the other three eligibles.

Situational uses:

- This coverage is good for taking away the inside receivers in a four-receiver set with double-coverage on each.
- This coverage is excellent against teams that throw vertical routes or seam routes with their inside receivers.
- Because of the outside leverage by the nickel and dime, this coverage is excellent when teams must get their receivers out of bounds to conserve the clock.

Strengths:

- Because of safeties' inside leverage deep, it is an excellent coverage against the post route.
- Defenders may overplay routes without fear of getting beat (e.g., post, post-corner)
- Strong versus outside-breaking routes
- Strong versus dig routes (down and in)
- Two receivers are being double-covered.
- Strong versus smash routes

Weaknesses:

- Difficult for safety to help on quick slant
- The linebacker and corners are in single coverage, with no help deep.
- Vulnerable to swing passes when the other receivers run deep; the linebacker has no help.
- Secondary run support is limited because the defensive backs are in man coverage and may have their backs turned to the quarterback when in press coverage.
- Only a four-man rush, with five offensive linemen to block them

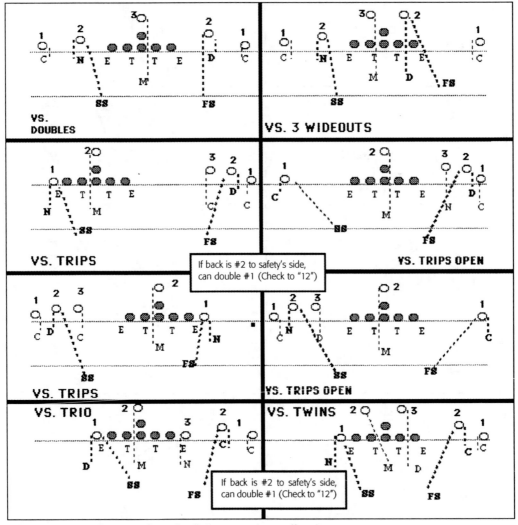

Diagram 7-15. Dime numbers "22" versus various offensive sets

Numbers "22" Bracket Drill

Numbers "22" Bracket Drill
Numbers "22" Technique

Safeties, Dime backs and Nickel backs practice bracket technique used in numbers "22" coverage vs. various routes. At the snap, the safety is at seven yards deep and 3–4 yards outside the #2 receiver. At the snap, the dime or Nickel is aligned with his outside side eye to the receiver's inside eye, playing inside press man technique. After running the drill with one side of the secondary, run the drill with both safeties and man defenders locked on the #2s.

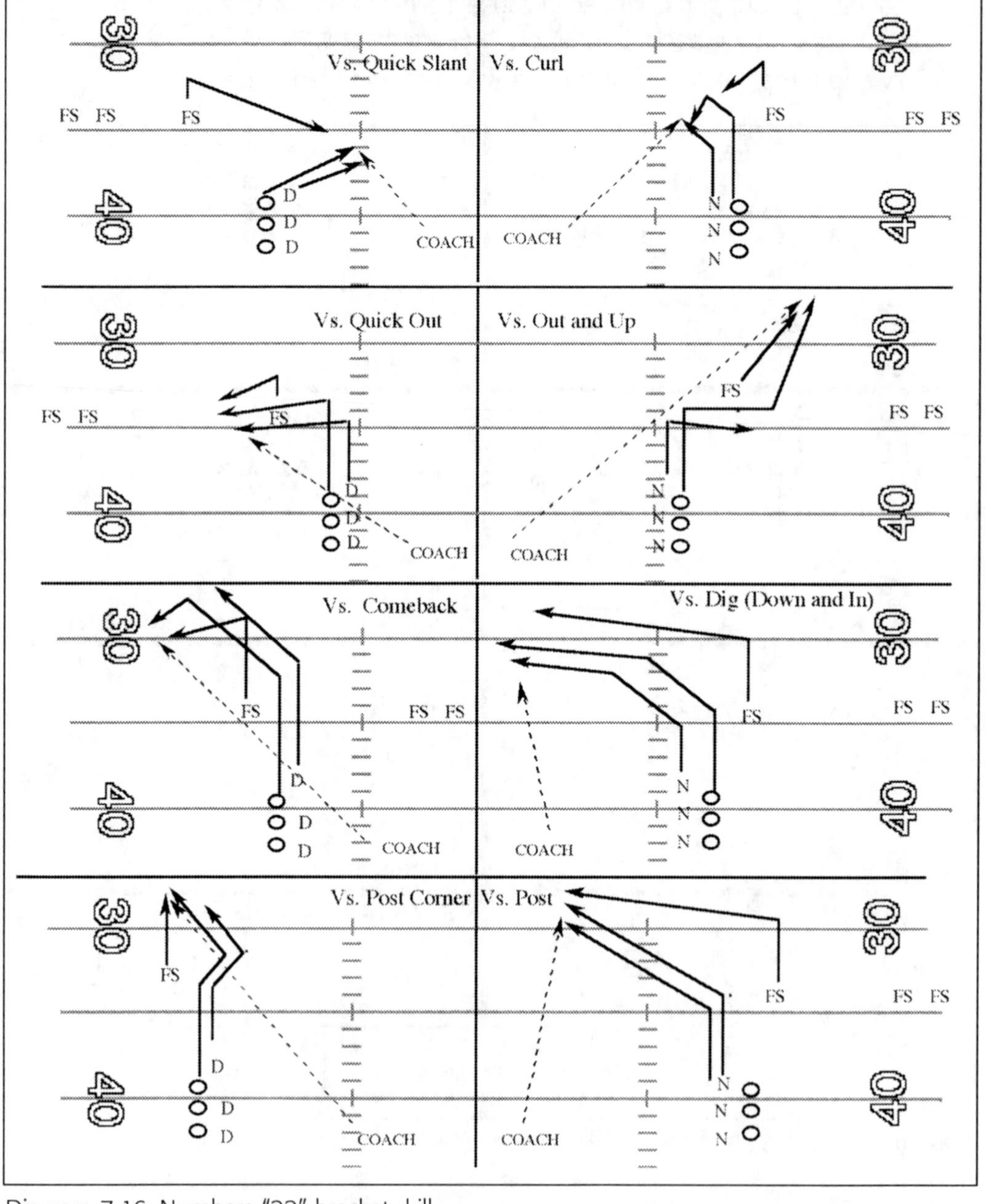

Vs. Quick Slant | Vs. Curl

Vs. Quick Out | Vs. Out and Up

Vs. Comeback | Vs. Dig (Down and In)

Vs. Post Corner | Vs. Post

Diagram 7-16. Numbers "22" bracket drill

Adjustment to Empty—Cover 1 Free Spy

Against any no-back (empty) formation or motion-to-empty formation versus man coverage, the 4-1-6 dime needs to be checked to "1 Free Spy." In this coverage, either the left or right safety would play man coverage on the fifth eligible, leaving the other safety to play free in the deep middle of the field. All numbers coverage (if called in the huddle) would be off. The Mike backer, who is normally responsible for the remaining back (fifth eligible), does not leave the box, because that would leave the defense vulnerable to a quarterback draw. Instead, the Mike backer plays a spy technique on the quarterback, anticipating the draw, and attacking the quarterback on any roll-out pass.

Situational uses:

- Adjustment to an offense that is motioning to empty (no backs)

Strengths:

- Provides a middle linebacker to stay in the box and defend the quarterback draw and short crossing routes
- Provides man coverage with a free safety
- Provides man coverage with a free safety who may double-cover one of the five receivers

Weaknesses:

- Eliminates the possibility of double-covering two receivers.

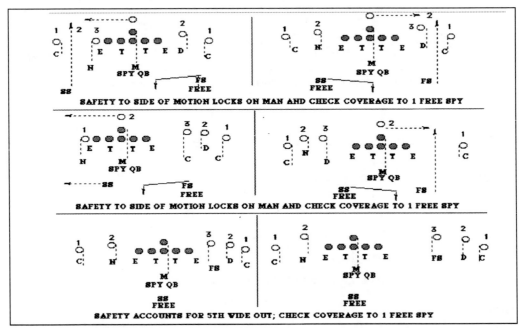

Diagram 7-17. Adjustment to empty—cover 1 free spy versus various offensive alignments

Dime Short Robber Cover 1 Free

One offensive strategy against a man-for-man defense is to clear the middle linebacker out of the short-middle zone by swinging the running back. Shallow slants, drags, and middle-return routes can then be run over the middle without fear of a middle linebacker interfering with the route. The defense may counter this strategy by using short-robber coverage. In a 4-1-6 dime, one of the two safeties (by a predetermined huddle call) will sprint to the middle-hook zone (i.e., 7 to 10 yards deep) at the snap of the ball. Then, he looks to break up any inside breaking routes by the receivers. If nothing shows immediately, he gains depth as quickly as possible, looking for a deeper crossing route. The other safety is free to react to the ball in the deep middle. The other four pass defenders are playing press-man technique (Diagram 7-18).

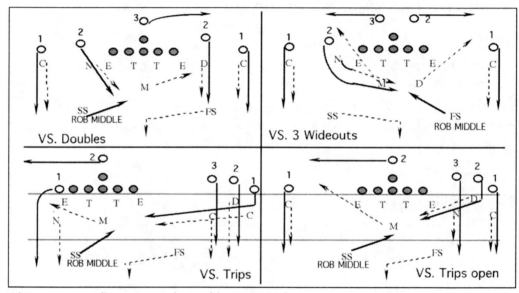

Diagram 7-18. Adjustment to short robber cover 1 free versus various offensive alignments

Situational uses:

- When running backs run pass routes, and coverage in the short hook (or middle) zone is desirable
- When slants and drags are expected

Strengths:

- Provides coverage for routes designed to exploit the void in the zone created by vacating middle linebackers
- Provides double-coverage on short-crossing routes

Weaknesses:

- Because one safety is used to play robber, only one safety is in deep coverage.

Dime Robber Cover 1 Free

One offensive strategy against a zone defense is to run multiple-level patterns. These patterns should include a shallow-crossing route (drag) in front of the linebackers, an intermediate route behind the linebackers in front of the safeties (deep in or dig), and a deep route (post) behind the safeties. The pattern is designed to draw the linebackers up to cover the shallow drag, and force the safeties to gain depth to cover the post. This scenario leaves a huge gap in the middle of the pass defense, anywhere from 15 to 18 yards deep, which is where the intermediate crossing route is run. It is extremely difficult for the middle linebacker to gain enough depth to be effective in covering the intermediate cross at 15 to 20 yards, especially if he sees the shallow-drag route and reacts to it. Also, in cover 2, a squat corner will not have sufficient depth in his drop to assist on anything but the shallow cross. Diagram 7-19 illustrates the squat corner's role in the dime robber cover 1 free.

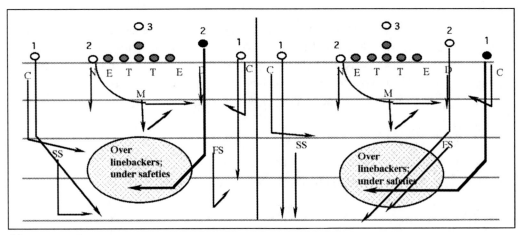

Diagram 7-19.

The defense may counter this strategy by using a robber coverage with man-free coverage. In a 4-1-6 dime, one of the two safeties (by a predetermined huddle call) will backpedal at a shallow angle toward the middle of the field to a point 15 to 17 yards deep. Then, he looks to break up any intermediate-crossing routes by the receivers. The other safety is free to react to the ball in the deep middle, covering a post route. The other four pass defenders are playing press-man technique (Diagram 7-20).

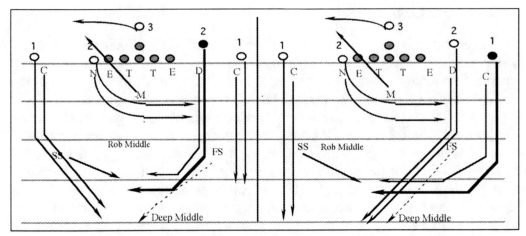

Diagram 7-20. The other four defenders are playing pres-man technique in a dime robber cover 1 free

Against a three-level pattern, the intermediate cross and the deep post are double-covered. The cross is covered by the defender in press-man technique and the safety robbing the middle. The post route is covered by the man in press technique and the safety who is free in coverage. Using robber coverage, the offensive advantage of the three-level (drag, dig, post) route is greatly diminished.

Situational uses:

- When multi-level crossing routes are expected
- When the drag, dig, post combination is expected

Strengths:

- Provides coverage for routes designed to exploit the void in the zone behind the linebackers and in front of the safeties
- Provides double-coverage on mid-level crossing routes

Weaknesses:

- Because one safety is used to play robber, only one safety is in deep coverage.

Dime Nitro Blitz

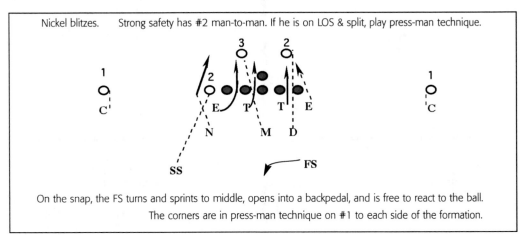

Diagram 7-21. Dime nitro blitz

Situational uses:

- Against a team that likes to send the tight end and back into the pass pattern
- Against a team that likes to roll out to the field
- Against a team that utilizes play-action to the strongside of the formation
- Against a team the utilizes a five- or seven-step drop by the quarterback
- Against a team that does not throw the fade well

Strengths:

- Five-man rush
- The quarterback should have to get rid of the ball quickly.
- Strong versus play-action
- Strong versus a roll-out to the strongside of the formation
- Man coverage with a free safety

Weaknesses:

- Off-tackle play to the strongside
- The tight end drag is difficult to cover unless the safety is aligned five to seven yards deep at the snap.
- The Mike backer may have difficulty covering a swing pass to the back.

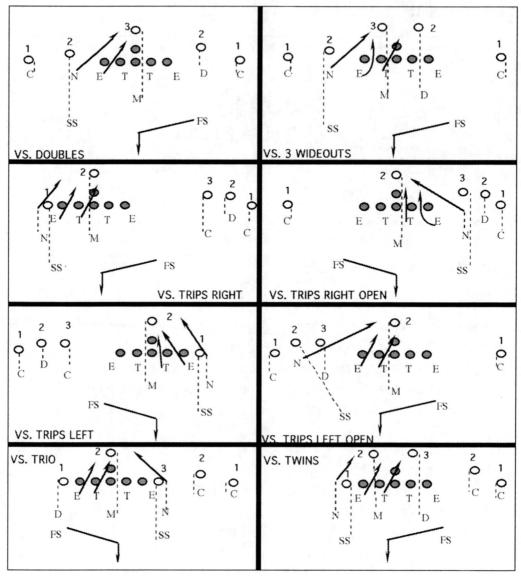

Diagram 7-22. Dime nitro blitz versus various offensive formations

4-1-6 Doom Blitz

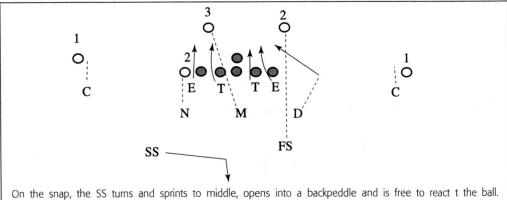

On the snap, the SS turns and sprints to middle, opens into a backpeddle and is free to react t the ball. The corners are in press man technique on #1 to each side of formation.

Diagram 7-23. 4-1-6 doom blitz

Situational uses:

- Against a team that sends the #2 receiver weak into the pass patterns
- Against a team that likes to bootleg
- Against a team that utilizes play-action to the weakside of the formation
- Against a team that utilizes a five- or seven-step drop by the quarterback
- Against a team that does not throw the fade well

Strengths:

- Five-man rush
- Strong versus bootleg
- The quarterback should have to get rid of the ball quickly.
- Strong versus play-action
- Strong versus a roll-out to the weakside of the formation
- Man coverage with a safety in deep coverage

Weaknesses:

- No safety help for the corners or nickel back
- The tight end drag is difficult to cover unless the nickel is aligned head-up five-to-seven yards deep at the snap.
- It is difficult for the Mike backer to cover the swing pass to the back.
- A screen to the strongside is difficult to cover.

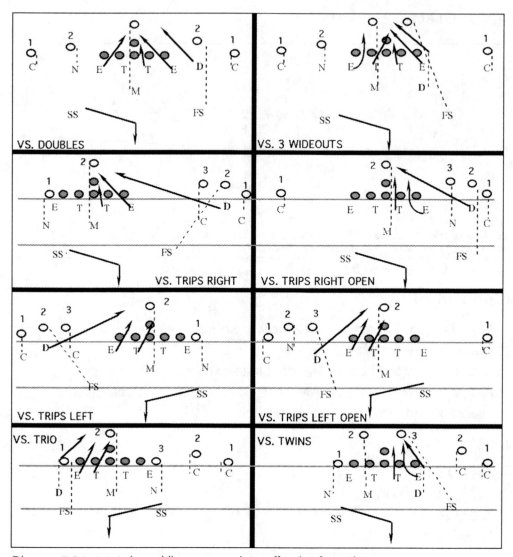

Diagram 7-24. 4-1-6 doom blitz versus various offensive formations

Dime Storm Blitz

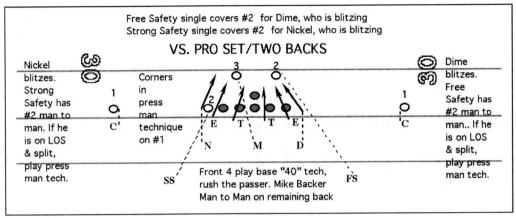

Diagram 7-25. Dime storm blitz

Situational uses:

- Against a team that likes to send the tight end and one or more backs into the pass pattern
- Against a team that utilizes a five- or seven-step drop by the quarterback
- Against a team that runs play-action
- Against a team that runs bootleg
- Against a team that rolls out to either side of the formation

Strengths:

- Seven-man rush
- The quarterback should have to get rid of the ball quickly.
- Strong versus play-action
- Strong versus a roll-out
- Strong versus bootleg

Weaknesses:

- Man-for-man defenders have no help.
- The Mike backer may have difficulty covering a swing pass to the back.
- The tight end drag is difficult to cover unless the safety is aligned five-to-seven yards deep at the snap.

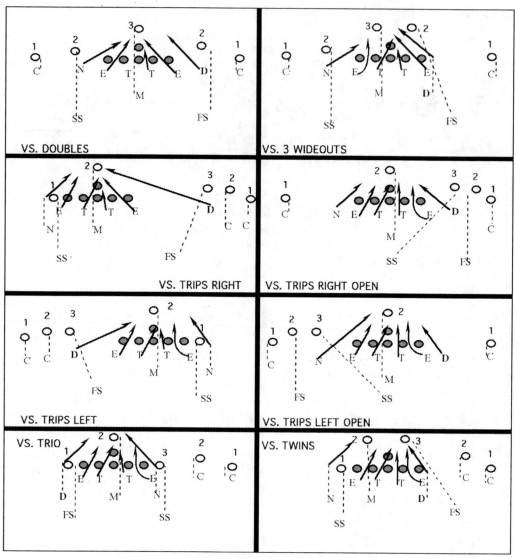

Diagram 7-26. Dime storm blitz versus various offensive formations

Dime Lightning Blitz

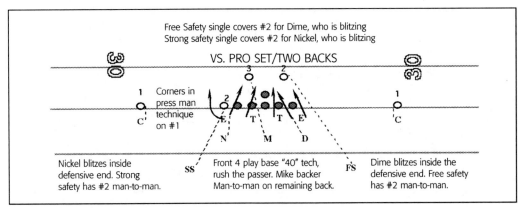

Diagram 7-27. Dime lightning blitz

Situational uses:

- Against a team that likes to send the tight end and backs into the pass pattern
- Against a team that utilizes a five- or seven-step drop by the quarterback
- Against a team that runs play-action

Strengths:

- Seven-man rush
- The quarterback should have to get rid of the ball quickly.
- Strong versus play-action

Weaknesses:

- Man-for-man defenders have no help.
- The Mike backer may have difficulty covering a swing pass to the back.
- The tight end drag is difficult to cover unless the safety is aligned five-to-seven yards deep at the snap.

Dime 3-Deep Zone Blitz

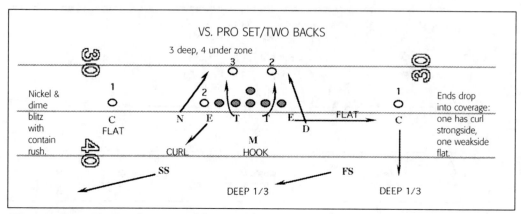

Diagram 7-28. Dime 3-deep zone blitz

Situational uses:

- Against a team that throws predictable hot routes.
- As a change-up to a blitz with man coverage
- In a long-yardage situation, when the quarterback will throw hot with short routes to the flats or over the middle.

Strengths:

- Four-man pass rush
- Disguised easily by normal alignment
- The quarterback is uncertain about which defenders are rushing and which are dropping into coverage.
- The strong end drops in the hot route area.
- A jam on the outside receiver prevents a clean release off the ball.
- The zone defenders can see the ball quickly and rally to the ball.

Dime Three-Deep Zone Blitz Versus Various Offensive Formations

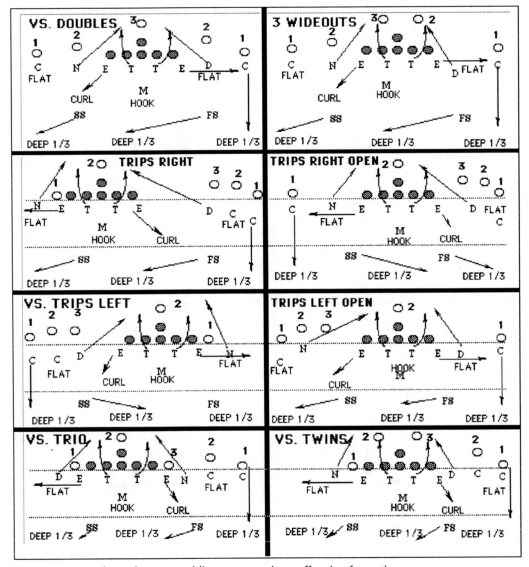

Diagram 7-29. Three-deep zone blitz versus various offensive formations

Dime Two-Deep Zone Blitz Versus Various Offensive Formations

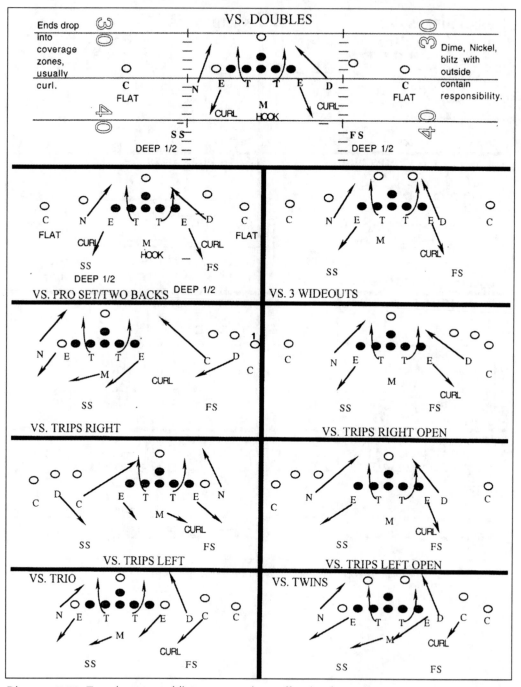

Diagram 7-30. Two-deep zone blitz versus various offensive formations

8

3-2-6 Dime Versus the Spread Offense

3-2-6 Dime Defense

| C – Cornerbacks |
| N – Nickel |
| D – Dime |
| S – Safeties |
| E – Ends |
| N – Nose |
| B – Inside Linebackers |

Diagram 8-1. Personnel in the 3-2-6 dime defense

The 3-2-6 dime is played with three down linemen, two middle linebackers, and six defensive backs. Usually, the defensive backs include two corners, two safeties, a nickel back, and a dime back. As a general rule, the nickel and dime backs replace one linebacker and one down lineman.

Situational uses:

- Against an offense that throws the ball with four or five receivers most of the time.
- On obvious passing downs
- To play double-coverage on one or more receivers
- As a prevent defense to eliminate the big play

Strengths:
- Two middle linebackers versus run plays

- Matches speed for speed by using two extra defensive backs
- Ability to double-cover one or more of the offense's receivers at any time
- Ability to blitz a linebacker or any of the six defensive backs with a free safety
- Ability to play robber coverage with a free safety
- Ability to play two-deep, three-deep, or four-deep coverage

Weakness:

- Five-in-the-box for inside runs

3-2-6 DIME NUMBERS FRONT & GAP RESPONSIBILIY CHART						
			BASIC RESPONSIBILITIES			
POSITION	ALIGN.	TECHNIQUE	RUN TO	RUN AWAY	KEY	DROPBACK PASS
LEFT END	OUTSIDE EYE OT	SQUEEZE 5 TECH.	C GAP IF M/M, FORCE	BOOTLEG REVERSE	BALL TO OT	CONTAIN RUSH OR STUNT
NOSE	HEAD UP CENTER	2 GAP	A GAPS	CUTBACK PURSUIT	BALL TO G-C-G COMBO	TWO WAY GO UNLESS STUNT
RIGHT END	OUTSIDE EYE OT	SQUEEZE 5 TECH.	C GAP IF M/M, FORCE	BOOTLEG REVERSE	BALL TO OT	CONTAIN RUSH OR STUNT
STRONG INSIDE LB	STACK STRONG GUARD	SQUEEZE HAT READ	B GAP	CUTBACK PURSUIT	STRONG GUARD	COVER CALL: MAN/ZONE BLITZ/COMBO
WEAK INSIDE LB	STACK WEAK GUARD	SQUEEZE HAT READ	B GAP	CUTBACK PURSUIT	STRONG GUARD	COVER CALL: MAN/ZONE BLITZ/COMBO
NICKEL	#2 STR OR TRIPS 3 WEAK	MAN/ZONE, BLITZ, OR DBL COVER	IF ZONE, FORCE	CUTBACK PURSUIT	ZONE-UNIT END TO #2; M/M - #2	COVER CALL: MAN/ZONE BLITZ/COMBO
DIME	#2 STR OR TRIPS 3 WEAK	MAN/ZONE, BLITZ, OR DBL COVER	IF ZONE, FORCE	CUTBACK PURSUIT	ZONE-UNIT END TO #2; M/M - #2	COVER CALL: MAN/ZONE BLITZ/COMBO
FREE SAFETY	PRE-SNAP 10-12 OFF LOS	MAN-FREE ZONE DBL COVER	INSIDE-OUT SUPPORT	CUTBACK PURSUIT	ONSIDE OG TO QB IN M/M, REC	COVER CALL: MAN/ZONE COVER FOR BLITZER
STRONG SAFETY	2 STRONG OR TRIPS 3 WEAK	MAN/ZONE, BLITZ, OR DBL COVER	IF ZONE, FORCE	CUTBACK PURSUIT	ZONE-UNIT END TO #2; M/M - #2	COVER CALL: MAN/ZONE BLITZ/COMBO
WEAK CORNER	1 STRONG #2 ST TWINS #3 ST TRIPS	MAN/ZONE OR DOUBLE COVER	PITCH PASS LATE ON SUPPORT	PITCH PASS LATE ON SUPPORT	ZONE-UNIT END TO QB; MAN-REC	COVER CALL: MAN/ZONE OR DBL COVER
STRONG CORNER	1 STRONG #2 WK TWINS #3 WK TRIPS	MAN/ZONE OR DOUBLE COVER	PITCH PASS LATE ON SUPPORT	PITCH PASS LATE ON SUPPORT	ZONE-UNIT END TO QB; MAN-REC	COVER CALL: MAN/ZONE OR DBL COVER

NOTE: ALIGNMENT OF DEFENSIVE BACKS ON ASSIGNED RECEIVERS DEPENDS ON COVER CALL

Diagram 8-2. 3-2-6 dime numbers front and gap responsibility chart

3-2-6 Dime Storm Blitz

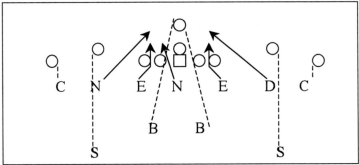

Diagram 8-3. 3-2-6 dime storm blitz

- The nickel and dime contain-blitz to their respective sides.
- The corners are in press-man technique.
- The linebackers have the back out to their side.
- The safeties are in man coverage on the slot receivers.
- The ends crash hard inside to the B gap.
- The nose aligns in a shade, either strong or weak.

Situational uses:

- Against teams that roll out to either side
- Against play-action
- Against a team that utilizes a five- or seven-step drop
- When blitzing off slot receivers

Strengths:

- May be run with #2 receivers in the slots
- Five-man rush
- The quarterback must get rid of the ball quickly.
- Strong versus flood routes
- Strong versus a roll-out
- Strong versus a play-action pass
- Safety covers for blitzing defenders
- Inside linebackers bracketing #3.
- The blitz is easily disguised.

Weakness:

- In a two-back set, a strongside pass route by the back is difficult for the safety to cover.

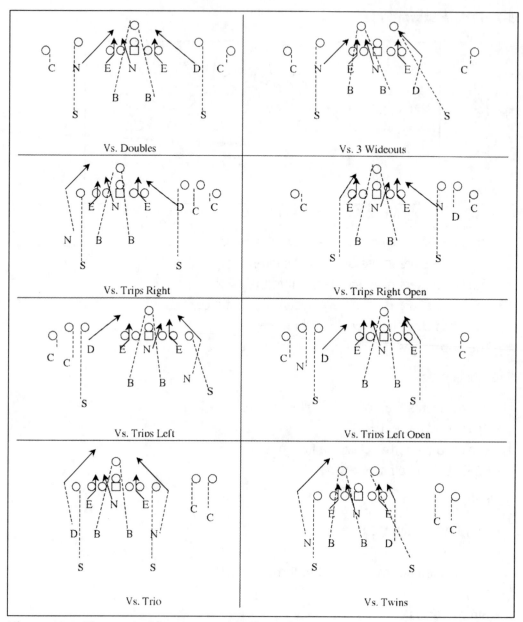

Diagram 8-4. Dime storm blitz versus various formations

3-2-6 Dime Doom Blitz

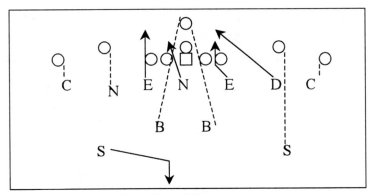

Diagram 8-5. 3-2-6 dime doom blitz

- The dime contain-blitzes.
- The nickel has man coverage on the slot.
- The corners are in press-man technique.
- The linebackers have the back out to their side.
- The safety is the adjuster for the dime; plays man on the slot.
- The end to the dime blitz side crashes hard into the B gap.
- The nose aligns in a shade, either strong or weak.
- The safety away from the blitz drops to the deep middle.

Situational uses:

- Against teams that roll out to their left
- Against play-action
- Against a team that utilizes a five- or seven-step drop
- When blitzing off a slot receiver

Strengths:

- May be run versus any set; if the dime blitzes, the free safety covers for him.
- Four-man rush
- Strong versus flood routes
- Strong versus a roll-out to the defensive right
- Strong versus a play-action pass
- The blitz is easily disguised.
- The inside linebackers are bracketing back.
- The man defenders have free-safety help.

Weakness:

- In a two-back set, it is difficult for the free safety to cover the back to his side if the back runs a pass route to the strongside of the set.

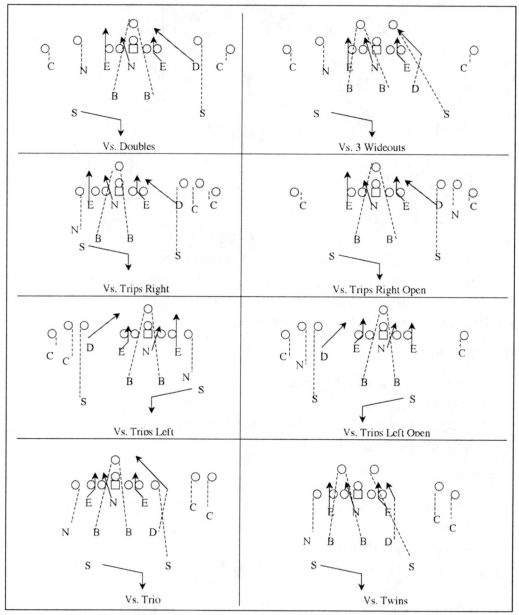

Diagram 8-6. Dime doom blitz versus various formations

3-2-6 Dime Nitro Blitz

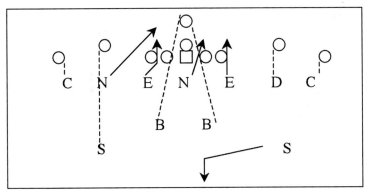

Diagram 8-7. 3-2-6 dime nitro blitz

- The nickel contain-blitzes.
- The dime has man coverage on the slot.
- The corners are in press-man technique.
- The linebackers have the back out to their side.
- The safety is the adjuster for the nickel; plays man coverage on the slot.
- The end to the nickel blitz side crashes hard into the B gap.
- The nose aligns in a shade, either strong or weak.
- The safety away from the blitz drops to the deep middle.

Situational uses:

- Against teams that roll out to their right
- Against play-action.
- Against a team that utilizes a five- or seven-step drop
- When blitzing off a slot receiver

Strengths:

- May be run versus any set; the nickel blitzes, and the strong safety covers for him.
- Four-man rush
- Strong versus flood routes
- Strong versus a roll-out
- Strong versus a play-action pass
- The blitz is easily disguised.
- The inside linebackers are bracketing back.
- The man defenders have free-safety help.

Weakness:

- A quick out by the tight end is difficult for the safety to cover unless at the snap, he is aligned head-up five-to-seven yards off the tight end.

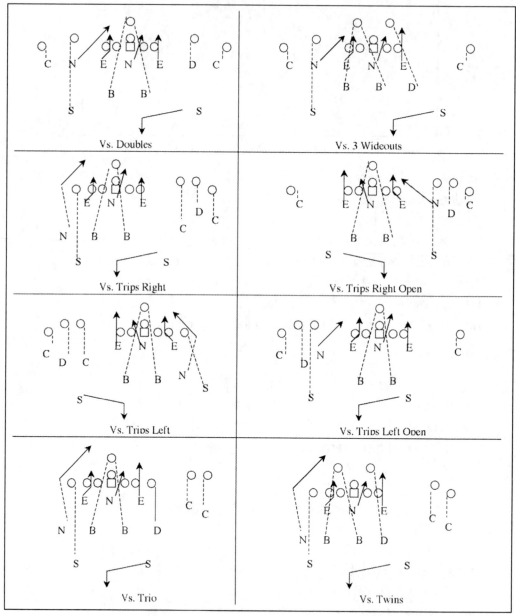

Diagram 8-8. Dime nitro blitz versus various formations

3-2-6 Dime Win Blitz

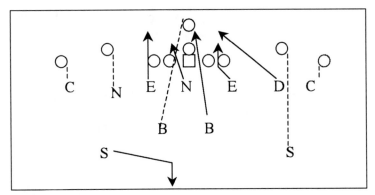

Diagram 8-9. 3-2-6 dime win blitz

- The dime contain-blitzes; the inside linebacker to the same side blitzes the A gap.
- The end to the blitz side crashed hard into the B gap.
- The nose crosses the face of the center into the strong A gap.
- The safety to the blitz side plays man coverage on the slot.
- The corners are in press-man technique.
- The nickel is in press-man technique on the slot.
- The non-blitzing linebacker has man coverage on the single back.
- The safety away from the blitz drops to the deep middle.

Situational uses:

- Against teams that roll out to their left
- Against play-action
- Against a team that utilizes a five- or seven-step drop
- When blitzing off a slot receiver

Strengths:

- May be run versus any set with the weak inside linebacker blitzing inside; the dime contain-blitzes, and the free safety covers for him.
- Five-man rush
- Strong versus flood routes
- Strong versus a roll-out to the defensive right
- Strong versus a play-action pass
- The blitz is easily disguised.
- The man defenders have free-safety help.

Weakness:

- In a two-back set, it is difficult for the free safety to cover the back to his side if the back runs a pass route to the strongside of the set.

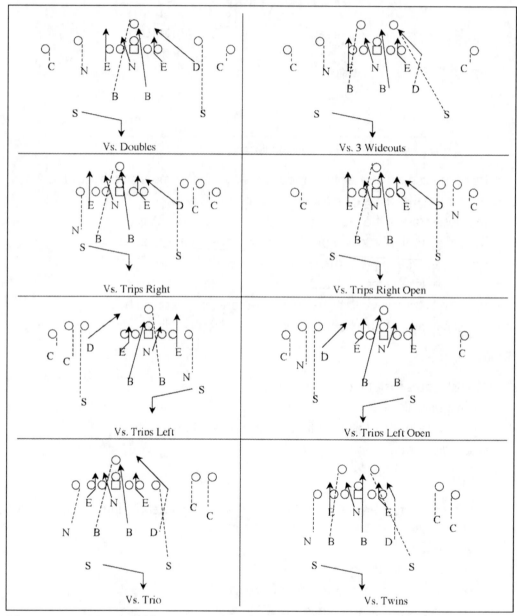

Diagram 8-10. Dime win blitz versus various formations

3-2-6 Dime Lightning Blitz

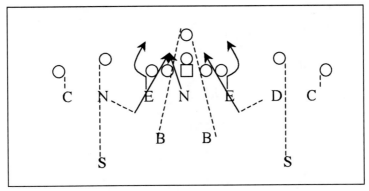

Diagram 8-11. 3-2-6 dime lightning blitz

- The nickel and time contain-blitz to their respective B gaps.
- The safeties are in man coverage on the slot receivers.
- The corners are in press-man technique.
- The linebackers have the back out to their side; they may bluff blitzing to occupy the offensive guards' attention.
- The ends attack the outside shoulder of the tackles and contain the rush.
- The nose aligns in a shade, either strong or weak.

Situational uses:

- Against a team that does not handle inside pressure particularly well
- Against a team that utilizes a five- or seven-step drop
- When a five-man rush is preferred

Strengths:

- Five-man rush
- The quarterback must get rid of the ball quickly.
- Strong versus flood routes
- The safety covers for blitzing defenders.
- The inside linebackers are bracketing #3.
- The blitz is easily disguised.

Weaknesses:

- Five blockers to block five defenders for run play versus spread sets
- A strongside pass route by the back is difficult for the free safety to cover.

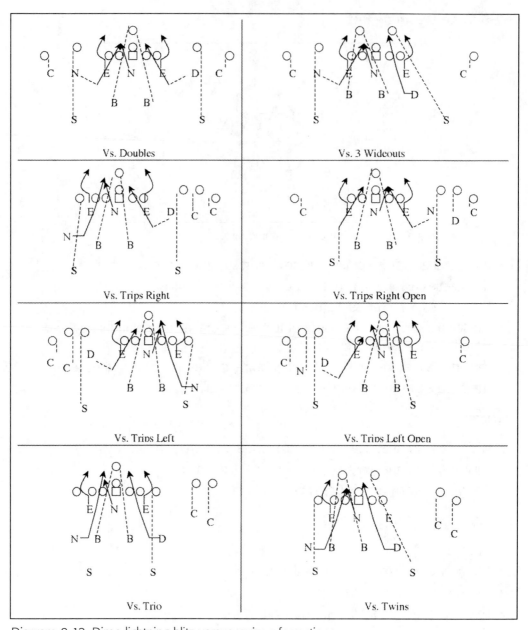

Diagram 8-12. Dime lightning blitz versus various formations

3-2-6 Dime Strike Blitz

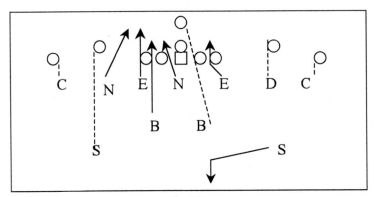

Diagram 8-13. 3-2-6 dime strike blitz

- The nickel contain-blitzes; the inside linebacker to the same side blitzes the B gap.
- The end to the blitz side bull rushes the offensive tackle.
- The nose crosses the face of the center into the strong A gap.
- The safety to the blitz side has man coverage on the slot.
- The corners are in press-man technique.
- The dime is in press-man technique on the slot.
- The non-blitzing linebacker has man coverage on the single back.
- The safety away from the blitz drops to the deep middle.

Situational uses:

- Against teams that roll out to their right
- Against play-action
- Against a team that utilizes a five- or seven-step drop
- When blitzing off a slot receiver

Strengths:

- May be run versus any set with the strong inside linebacker blitzing inside; the nickel contain-blitzes, and the strong safety covers for him.
- Five-man rush
- Strong versus flood routes
- Strong versus a roll-out to the defensive left
- Strong versus a play-action pass
- The blitz is easily disguised.
- The man defenders have free-safety help.

Weakness:

- In a two-back set, it is difficult for the weak-inside linebacker to cover the back to his side if the back runs a pass route to the strongside of the set.

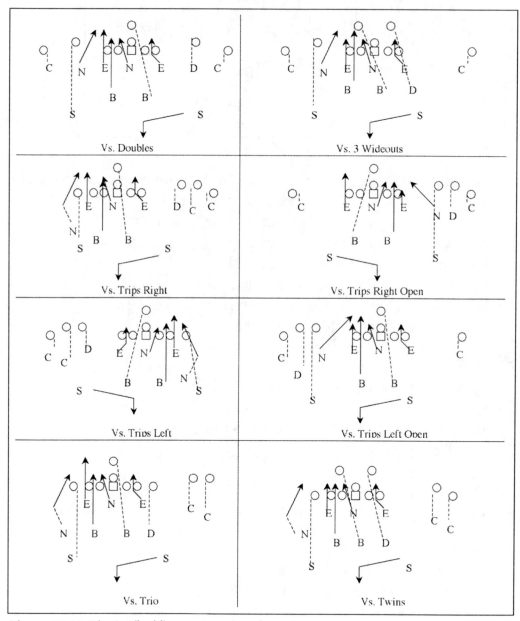

Diagram 8-14. Dime strike blitz versus various formations

3-2-6 Dime Double Plug 1 Robber

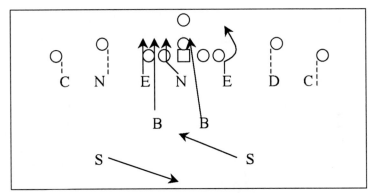

Diagram 8-15. 3-2-6 dime double plug 1 robber

- The nickel and dime are in press technique on the slot.
- The corners are in pres-man technique.
- The strongside linebacker blitzes the strong B gap.
- The weakside linebacker blitzes the weak A gap.
- The nose uses a rip technique to attack the strongside guard.
- The ends contain the rush.
- The weakside safety is responsible for short to mid-level crossing routes.
- The opposite safety is responsible for the deep middle.

Situational uses:

- Against teams that do not handle inside pressing particularly well
- Against play-action
- Against a team that utilizes a five- or seven-step drop
- Against teams that throw hot routes in the middle-hook zone
- When double-coverage is preferred on at least one receiver

Strengths:

- Five-man rush
- Inside pressure
- Man coverage with a free safety
- Robber denies short-crossing routes.
- The quarterback must get rid of the ball quickly.
- Strong versus flood routes
- Strong versus a play-action pass
- The blitz is easily disguised.

Weaknesses:

- The right end is in a blitz-peel technique if the back to his side swings.
- In a two-back set, a strongside pass route by the back to his side is difficult for the dime to cover.

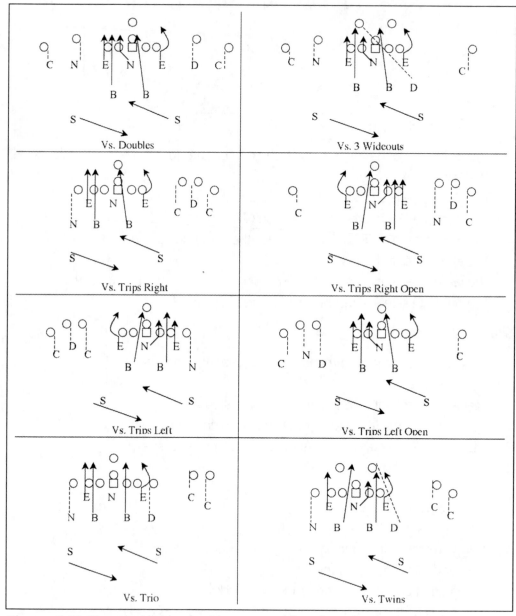

Diagram 8-16. Dime double plug 1 robber versus various formations

3-2-6 Dime Field Slam 1 Free

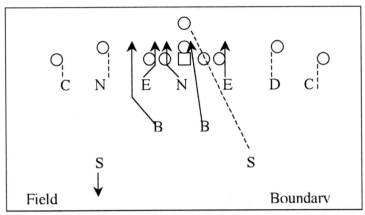

Diagram 8-17. 3-2-6 dime field slam 1 free

- The corners, nickel, and dime are in press-man coverage.
- The end to the field-side crashes into the B gap; the end to the boundary contains the rush.
- The nose uses a rip technique to attack the field-side guard.
- The linebacker to the field-side contain-blitzes through the C gap.
- The linebacker to the boundary-side blitzes through the weakside A gap.
- The safety to the field-side drops to the middle of the field.
- The safety to the boundary-side is in man coverage on the single back.

Situational uses:

- Against teams that roll out to the field
- Against play-action
- Against a team that utilizes a five- or seven-step drop
- Against a team that runs flood routes to the field

Strengths:

- Five-man rush
- The quarterback must get rid of the ball quickly.
- Strong versus a roll-out
- Strong versus a play-action pass
- Strong versus flood routes
- The blitz is easily disguised.
- Man coverage with a free safety

Weakness:

- In a one- or two-back set, a pass route by #3 into the boundary will be difficult to cover.

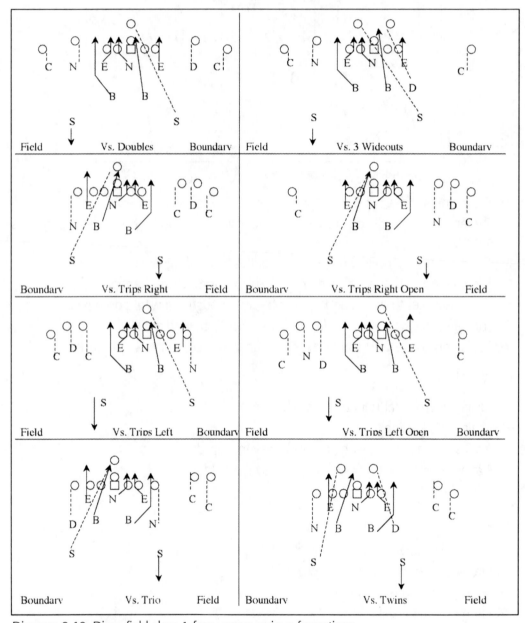

Diagram 8-18. Dime field slam 1 free versus various formations

3-2-6 Dime Fire Weak Blitz

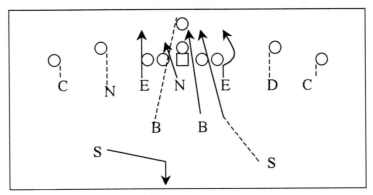

Diagram 8-19. 3-2-6 dime fire weak blitz

- The corners, nickel, and dime are in press-man technique.
- The ends have contain rush.
- The nose attacks the strong A gap.
- The free safety blitzes the weak B gap.
- The weakside linebacker blitzes the weak A gap.
- The strongside linebacker has man coverage on the remaining back.
- The strongside safety drops to the deep middle.

Situational uses:

- Against teams that utilize one-back sets on passing downs
- Against a team that utilizes a five- or seven-step drop
- Against teams that do not handle inside pressure particularly well

Strengths:

- Five-man rush
- The quarterback must get rid of the ball quickly.
- Man coverage with free-safety help
- Strong inside pressure weakside

Weaknesses:

- A swing pass to the remaining back away from the inside linebacker is difficult to cover.
- Difficult to disguise well

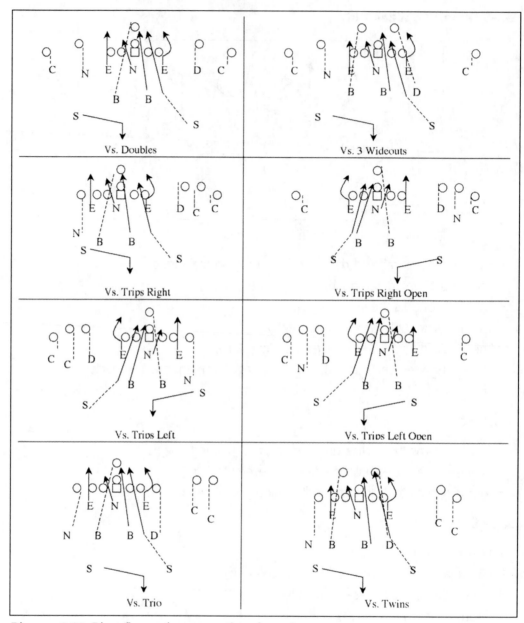

Diagram 8-20. Dime fire weak versus various formations

3-2-6 Dime Double Fire Zone Blitz

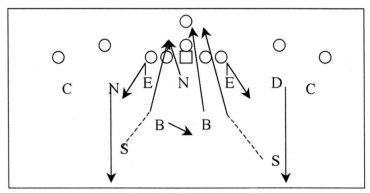

Diagram 8-21. 3-2-6 dime double fire zone blitz

- The corners are in a squat technique in the flats.
- The nickel and dime drop to the deep halves.
- The ends engage the offensive tackles and drop to the curl zones.
- The nose attacks the strong A gap.
- The weakside linebacker blitzes the weak A gap.
- The strongside linebacker drops to the middle hook.
- The safeties blitz respective to their B gaps.

Situational uses:

- As a change-up to mix in with traditional blitzes with man coverage
- Against a quarterback who throws hot well versus man blitzes
- Against a team that uses one-back formations on passing downs
- When a two-deep zone with inside pressure is desirable

Strengths:

- Four-man rush
- The squat corners jam the receivers off the line, preventing their free release.
- Their quarterback is unsure who is blitzing and who is dropping into coverage.
- The quarterback must get rid of the ball quickly.
- Strong versus common hot routes in man blitzes
- Seven defenders are in zone pass coverage (two-deep, five underneath).

Weakness:

- No jam on the #2 receivers

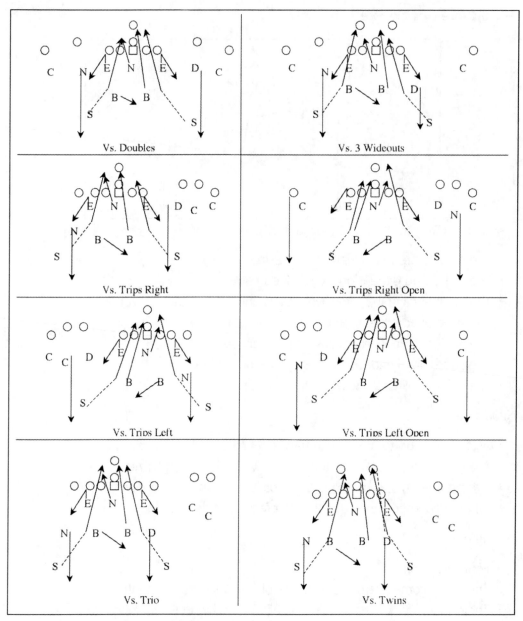

Diagram 8-22. Dime fire zone blitz versus various formations

3-2-6 Dime Tornado Blitz

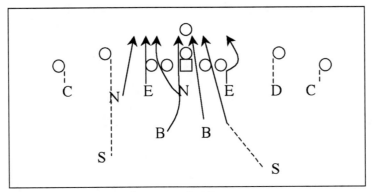

Diagram 8-23. 3-2-6 dime tornado blitz

- The corners and dime are in man-press technique.
- The nickel contains the rush.
- The safety to the nickel-side has man coverage on the slot.
- The weak safety blitzes the weak B gap.
- The weakside linebacker blitzes the weak A gap.
- The strongside linebacker blitzes the strong A gap.
- The strongside end bull rushes the offensive tackle.
- The nose uses a rip technique and attacks the strongside offensive guard.

Situational use:

- When maximum pressure on the quarterback is desirable

Strengths:

- Seven-man rush
- The quarterback should not have much time to get rid of the ball.
- Strong versus play-action
- Strong versus a roll-out
- Strong versus teams that utilize a five- or seven-step drop

Weaknesses:

- Man-to-man defenders have no safety help.
- The nickel and end must use a blitz-peel technique if the backs swing.

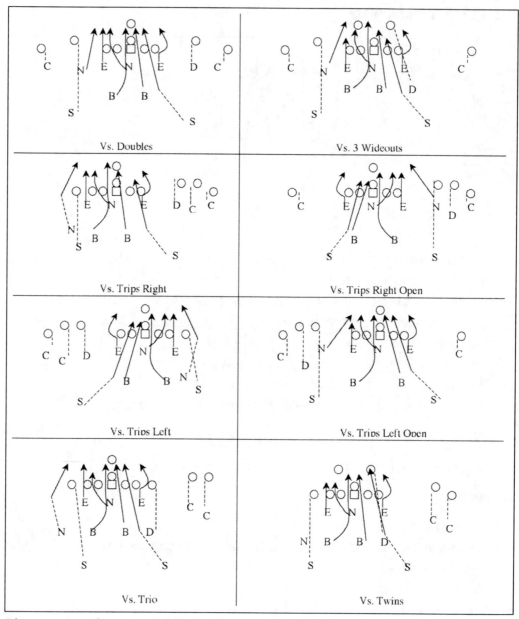

Diagram 8-24. Dime tornado blitz versus various offensive formations

9

The 4-3 Defense Versus the Spread Offense

The 4-3 defense is an excellent defense to defend the spread because of its versatility. Adjustments can be made to handle a wide variety of spread formations, as well as an "ace" formation, which includes two tight ends, one back, and two wide receivers that many spread teams employ. A multitude of coverages are also possible. Diagram 9-1 illustrates the many pass coverages that are possible from a cover 2 shell, a cover 3 shell, and a cover 0 shell.

Strengths:

- Multitude of zone, man, and combination coverage possibilities
- Many front variations possible (college or pro 4-3)
- Ease of putting eight in the box versus two tight ends
- Several adjustments to spread formations
- Easy to drop seven or eight into pass coverage
- Easy to use safeties as adjusters when blitzing linebackers

Weaknesses:

- Less effective versus the run with a two-safety look
- Need a defensive back in the box versus two tight ends to be effective in stopping the run

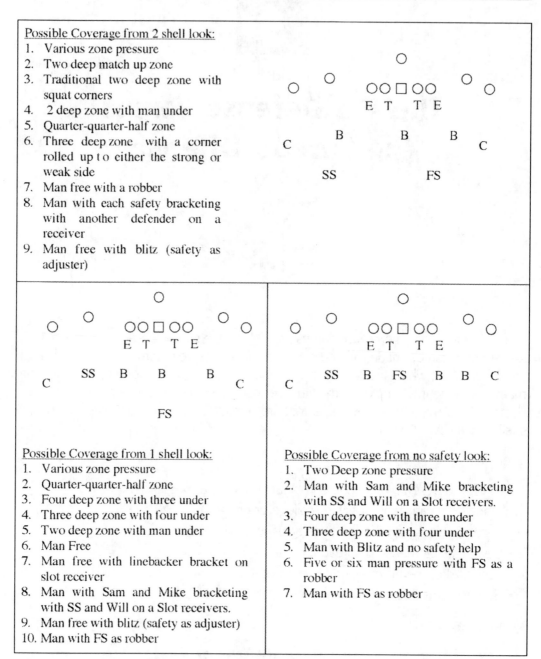

Possible Coverage from 2 shell look:
1. Various zone pressure
2. Two deep match up zone
3. Traditional two deep zone with squat corners
4. 2 deep zone with man under
5. Quarter-quarter-half zone
6. Three deep zone with a corner rolled up to either the strong or weak side
7. Man free with a robber
8. Man with each safety bracketing with another defender on a receiver
9. Man free with blitz (safety as adjuster)

Possible Coverage from 1 shell look:
1. Various zone pressure
2. Quarter-quarter-half zone
3. Four deep zone with three under
4. Three deep zone with four under
5. Two deep zone with man under
6. Man Free
7. Man free with linebacker bracket on slot receiver
8. Man with Sam and Mike bracketing with SS and Will on a Slot receivers.
9. Man free with blitz (safety as adjuster)
10. Man with FS as robber

Possible Coverage from no safety look:
1. Two Deep zone pressure
2. Man with Sam and Mike bracketing with SS and Will on a Slot receivers.
3. Four deep zone with three under
4. Three deep zone with four under
5. Man with Blitz and no safety help
6. Five or six man pressure with FS as a robber
7. Man with FS as robber

Diagram 9-1. Possible coverages with a 4-3 alignment

College 4-3 With a 3 Shell

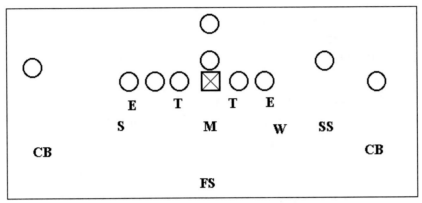

Diagram 9-2. 4-3 cover 3 shell versus tight end doubles formation

Strengths:

- Ability to play 3-deep zone
- Ability to play man-free with one or two linebackers blitzing
- Ability to play 4-deep zone coverage
- Seven-man front versus run
- Multiple-front adjustments possible

Weaknesses:

- A man short versus two tight ends, unless a safety is brought up into the box
- Vulnerable to the trapping game

Front Adjustments:

Diagrams 9-3 to 9-6 illustrate several 4-3 front adjustments that may be utilized.

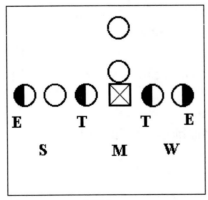

Diagram 9-3. "G" front

Strengths:

- Ability to bring four to seven pass rushers
- Seven-man front versus run
- Good adjustment versus teams with an outstanding center
- Strong versus option
- Strong versus weakside run
- The center has a difficult block on a quick Mike linebacker versus full-flow run plays.

Weaknesses:

- May be less effective versus strongside run
- Vulnerable to trapping game
- Zone blocking concepts present double-team opportunities for offensive linemen on the stretch play.

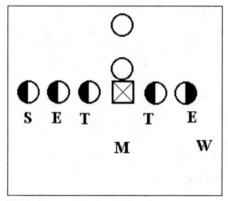

Diagram 9-4. "G" solid

Strengths:

- Effective versus strongside running game with four defenders to the strongside
- Ability to bring four to seven pass rushers
- Seven-man front versus run
- The center must help on a weakside tackle pinch, which allows the Mike linebacker to flow to the ball.
- Strong versus weakside run
- The center has a difficult block on a quick Mike linebacker on full-flow run plays.
- May require three-man zone blocking concept on strongside stretch play.
- Ability to play 3-deep zone
- Ability to play 2-deep, 5-under zone
- Ability to play 4-deep zone

Weaknesses:

- Vulnerable to the counter
- Vulnerable to the trapping game
- A big tight end may outmatch the Sam linebacker on the line of scrimmage.

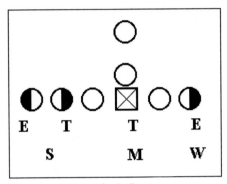

Diagram 9-5. Wide "G"

Strengths:

- The widened alignment of the defensive ends provides a better pass rush.
- Strong versus weakside run
- Ability to bring four to seven pass rushers
- Many stunt and blitz combinations easily executed from this alignment

Weaknesses:

- Zone-blocking concepts present double-team opportunities for offensive linemen on the stretch play.
- Vulnerable to draws if not disguised

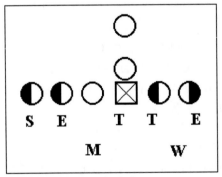

Diagram 9-6. Eagle "G"

Strengths:

- Seven-man front versus run
- Effective versus strongside running game with four defenders to the strongside
- Ability to bring four to seven pass rushers
- Strong versus weakside run with the Will linebacker covered up
- The center has a difficult single block on a quick, penetrating 1 technique, which may force a double-team with the guard.
- Ability to play 3-deep zone
- Ability to play 2-deep, 5-under zone
- Ability to play 4-deep zone
- Easy to bring three or four from the weakside

Weaknesses:

- Cutback on an inside zone play to the strongside if the weak tackle is flattened out or overpursues
- Weakside trap

4-3 Cover Two-Deep, Match-up Zone

The two-deep zone using match-up principles is an effective way to defend the spread offense. The execution of the zone is based on pattern reading, rather than traditional spot drops. Each of the seven defenders have specific reads and rules, which when executed, make this pass coverage very effective. The usual routes used by the spread offense to attack a two-deep zone are ineffective if defenders execute their assignments.

❑ Principles of the 4-3 two-deep, match-up zone:

- Disrupt the timing of the receivers and the quarterback.
- Give pass rushers more time to teach the quarterback.
- Take away the speed of the wide receivers.
- Protect the slower flat defenders (corners or ends).
- Understand that the linebackers are stretched and that the front is more effective versus pass than run.
- Use when better up front than the opposition and can stop the run with six in the box; also use in long-yardage situations.
- On second down and third-and-ten, be willing to give up four yards on an inside run at the expense of defending the perimeter and deep pass.
- Cover receivers, not spots. Recognize patterns as they develop and lock man-to-man on receivers, based on reads. Remember, "zone early, man late."

❑ Reads of the 4-3 two-deep, match-up zone

The corners have three reads:

- Smash route by #1—yell, "smash, smash, smash" and lock up with #1.
- Outside release by #1 (fade)—carry the route.
- Inside release by #1 up the field—yell, "in, in, in", carry #1's vertical and anticipate his break inside, and find #2 and lock up man with him.

The outside linebackers have four reads:

- #2 vertical with #1 vertical on the boundary—carry the vertical and defend the seam; stay between #2 and the quarterback.
- #2 vertical release upfield with #1 inside release—carry #2's vertical route, anticipating #1's break to the inside on the square-in; get underneath the square-in.
- #2 inside release (crosses the field in front of you). With no back to your side, backpedal straight back to get into position to defend a deep crossing route. With a back to your side, when #2 crosses in front of you, check the back coming out of the backfield; play him as if he lined up wide with all of the same rules.
- Outside release by #2—hunt #1, who will either curl up or run vertical; lock up with him.

Middle linebacker has four reads (no release, inside, outside, and vertical):

- If the back is #3, stay aligned over him, backpedal, and look for #2 to break inside. If #3 releases as a check-down outlet, rally up to him.
- If #3 releases outside and becomes #2, look to that side for the receiver who has just broken inside and become #3; lock up with him.
- If a trips set, run vertical with #3.
- If #3 crosses inside, jump the route.

The two safeties execute their traditional 2-deep zone responsibility, "keeping everything in front of them:"

- Read #2's (slot) release. If he releases vertically, continue backpedaling, and anticipate a seam route or a break to the corner in the smash route. In the case of four verticals, play the ball, because all four receivers should be covered by the corners and two outside linebackers (refer to the previous diagrams).
- If #2 releases outside and becomes #1, look to that side for the receiver who has just broken inside and become #2, continue to backpedal for depth, and anticipate a post. If the new #2 curls up (as in a flat/curl route), look quickly to see if the new #1 is threatening the deep half (flat-and-up route).

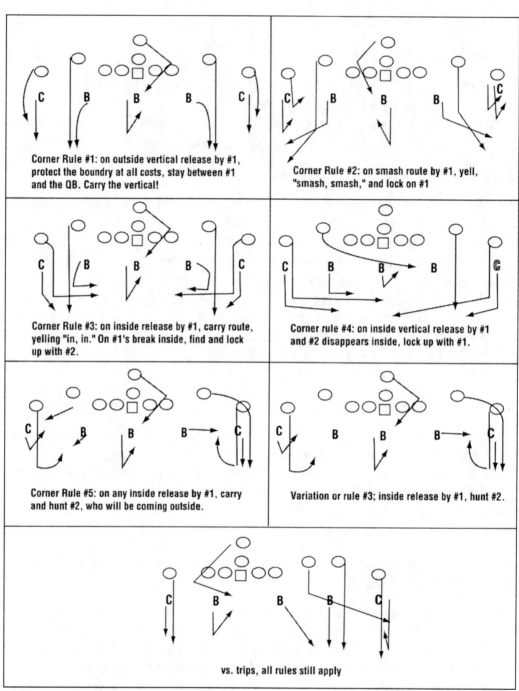

Corner Rule #1: on outside vertical release by #1, protect the boundry at all costs, stay between #1 and the QB. Carry the vertical!

Corner Rule #2: on smash route by #1, yell, "smash, smash," and lock on #1

Corner Rule #3: on inside release by #1, carry route, yelling "in, in." On #1's break inside, find and lock up with #2.

Corner rule #4: on inside vertical release by #1 and #2 disappears inside, lock up with #1.

Corner Rule #5: on any inside release by #1, carry and hunt #2, who will be coming outside.

Variation or rule #3; inside release by #1, hunt #2.

vs. trips, all rules still apply

Diagram 9-7. Corner reads in the 2-deep match-up zone

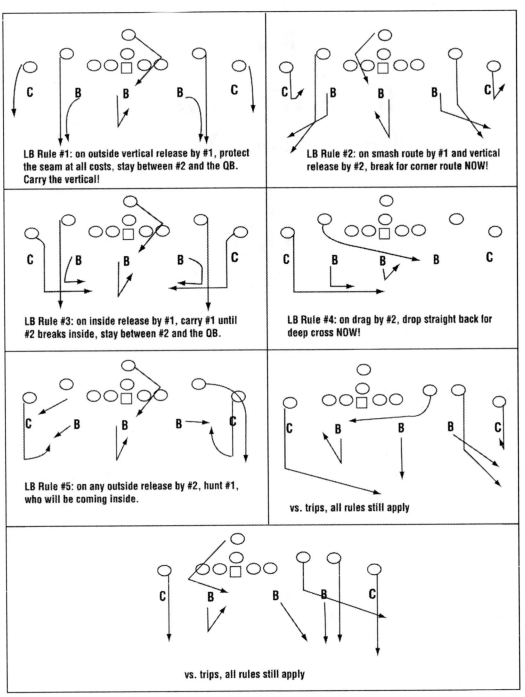

LB Rule #1: on outside vertical release by #1, protect the seam at all costs, stay between #2 and the QB. Carry the vertical!

LB Rule #2: on smash route by #1 and vertical release by #2, break for corner route NOW!

LB Rule #3: on inside release by #1, carry #1 until #2 breaks inside, stay between #2 and the QB.

LB Rule #4: on drag by #2, drop straight back for deep cross NOW!

LB Rule #5: on any outside release by #2, hunt #1, who will be coming inside.

vs. trips, all rules still apply

vs. trips, all rules still apply

Diagram 9-8. Outside linebacker reads in the 2-deep match-up zone

10

The 46 Nickel Versus the Spread Offense

46 Nickel Defense

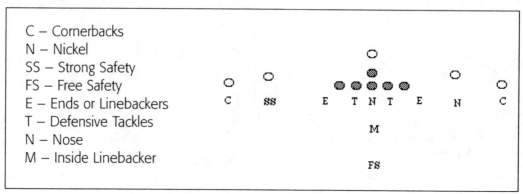

C – Cornerbacks
N – Nickel
SS – Strong Safety
FS – Free Safety
E – Ends or Linebackers
T – Defensive Tackles
N – Nose
M – Inside Linebacker

Diagram 10-1. Personnel in the 46 nickel defense

In recent years, a resurgence of the 46 defense at the high school, college, and professional levels has occurred. Rather than focusing on the installation or technique for the 46 defense, this chapter emphasizes a nickel package, with a wide variety of zones, combination coverage, man pressure, and zone pressure. Diagram 10-2 illustrates some base adjustments to spread formations.

Strengths:

• Easy formation adjustments versus the spread offense
• Excellent push up the center of the pass pocket
• Forces the tackles to block a speed rusher from the outside in big-on-big protection

- Multiple three-man games involving the nose and both defensive tackles can cause havoc with both man- and zone-blocking schemes.
- The middle linebacker is covered up.
- Five, six, or seven defenders can easily be sent at the quarterback.
- Various zone pressure easily utilized
- Various zone coverage (2-deep, 3-deep, 4-deep) easily utilized
- Various combination coverage easily utilized (single-bracket, double-bracket, and 2-deep man under versus two-back, three-wide formation)
- Difficult to trap against

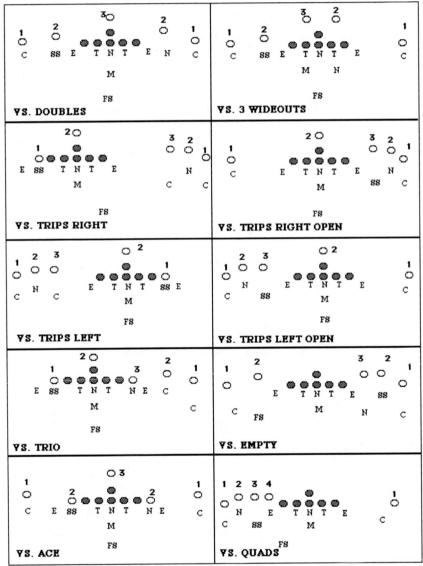

Diagram 10-2. 46 nickel versus various offensive formations

Weaknesses:

- Versus off-tackle plays
- Versus a sprint draw
- Versus a counter trey
- Pass routes that send a back down the seam of the field

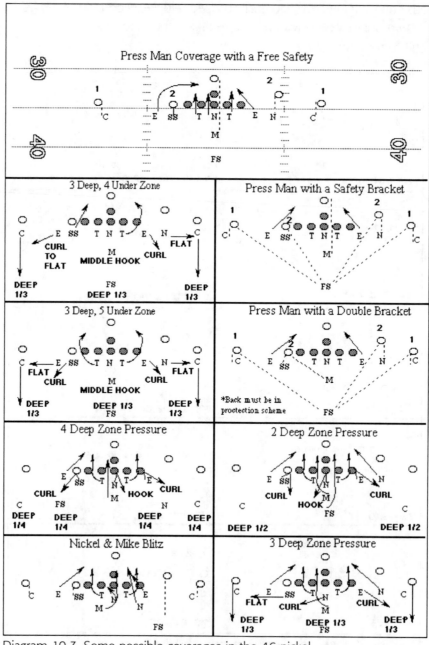

Diagram 10-3. Some possible coverages in the 46 nickel

46 Nickel Cover 1 Free

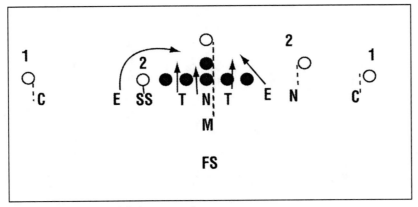

Diagram 10-4. 46 nickel cover 1 free

Situational Uses:

- Against man-on-man (big-on-big) pass protection
- Against a team with a good tight end who is used in pass routes
- When a jam on all receivers is desired
- Against a team that has one or more offensive tackles who can be beaten off the edge
- Against a team that runs a 90s (three-step, quick) passing game

Strengths:

- Five-man rush
- Free safety in deep coverage
- All receivers jammed off the line of scrimmage
- Quick contain rushers off the edge have an advantage against offensive tackles in man protection.
- Strong versus any roll-out pass
- Strong push up the middle by the nose and defensive tackles
- Easy to bring six (Mike), or seven (SS), with no pre-snap read

Weaknesses:

- Free safety unlikely to help on fade routes
- The Mike backer must hustle to get to a swing pass to the back.

46 Nickel Three-Deep, Five-Under Zone

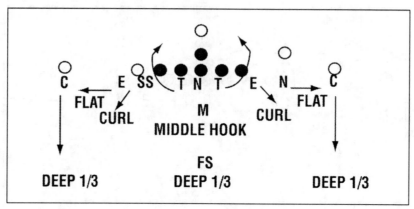

Diagram 10-5. 46 nickel three-deep, five-under zone

Situational Uses:

- When having eight defenders in pass coverage is desirable.
- Against a team that throws to the flats
- Against a team that swings the back, anticipating man coverage from the Mike
- Against a team that runs a 90s (three-step, quick) passing game

Strengths:

- Eight defenders in pass coverage
- Three-deep zone
- Sound versus 90s passing game
- A swing pass to back negated by flat defenders
- Strong versus the deep pass

Weakness:

- Three-man pass rush

46 Nickel Three-Deep Zone Pressure

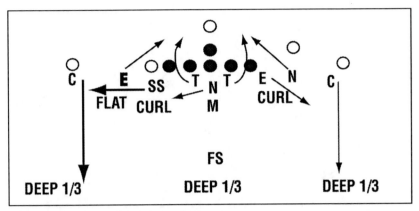

Diagram 10-6. 46 nickel three-deep zone pressure

Situational Uses:

- Against a team that throws predictable hot routes
- As a change-up to blitzing with man coverage
- Against a team that often throws to the flats

Strengths:

- The quarterback and linemen are uncertain as to who is rushing and who is dropping into coverage.
- Three-deep zone
- Seven in pass coverage
- Four-man rush
- The strong safety is often free with the element of surprise.

Weaknesses:

- A quick pass to the tight end down the seam
- The left defensive tackle must contain the rush.

46 Nickel Numbers (Double-Bracket)

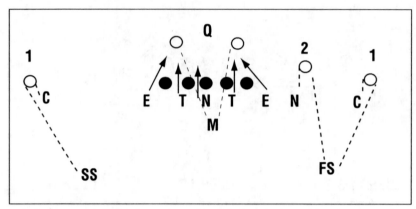

Diagram 10-7. 46 nickel numbers (double-bracket)

Versus a three-receiver formation, the nickel is the adjuster and would cross the formation and align on #2. When a two-digit number is called in the huddle or at the line of scrimmage, the first digit tells the left safety who to double to his side of the formation (#1 or #2), and the second digit tells the right safety who to double to his side of the formation (#1 or #2). For example, if the call was "numbers 11," each #1 receiver would be doubled by the corner and safety to his side. If "numbers 12" was called, the single receiver on the left would be doubled by the corner and safety to his side, and the #2 (slot) would be doubled by the nickel and safety to his side. If the call was "numbers 21," the nickel would double the slot with the safety, and the corner and safety would double the wide-out to the other side.

Situational Uses:

- Against a two-back, three-receiver formation in an obvious passing situation
- When an offense utilizes two backs in a max-protection scheme
- When double-coverage on two of the three receivers in the formation is desired.
- As a change-up to straight zone or man free

Strengths:

- Double-coverage on the two best receivers
- Five-man rush
- The quarterback should have to get rid of the ball quickly.
- Great versus 90s passing game, because the short passes are negated by press coverage
- Easily disguised as 2-deep zone, or 2-deep man-under

Weaknesses:

- The ends must use a peel technique and cover a back to their side if he releases into pattern.
- The middle linebacker responsible for covering either back down the seams.
- Single-man coverage on one of three receivers, with no safety help

Nickel Press-Man Coverage with a Double-Bracket

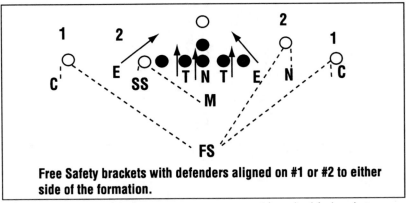

Free Safety brackets with defenders aligned on #1 or #2 to either side of the formation.

Diagram 10-8. 46 nickel press-man coverage with a double-bracket

Situational Uses:

- Against man-on-man (big-on-big) pass protection
- Against a team with a good tight end who is used in pass routes
- When double-coverage is desired on the tight end and one other receiver
- Against a team that has one or more offensive tackles who can be beaten off the edge
- When the back is expected to stay in for protection

Strengths:

- Five-man rush
- The free safety bracketing with either one of the corners or the nickel
- Quick-contain rushers off the edge have an advantage against offensive tackles in man protection.
- Strong versus any roll-out pass
- Strong push up the middle by the nose and defensive tackles
- Tight end bracketed by the strong safety and the Mike

Weaknesses:

- The rush ends must use a blitz-peel technique and cover a back if he releases to their side.
- The two pass defenders have no safety help.

46 Nickel Nickel and Mike Blitz

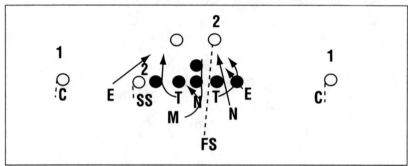

Diagram 10-9. 46 nickel nickel and Mike blitz

Situational Uses:

- Against man-on-man (big-on-big) pass protection
- Against a team with a good tight end who is used in pass routes
- To force a hot throw
- Against a team that uses their backs in pass protection

Strengths:

- Seven-man rush
- Four-man rush to the weakside of the formation
- The nickel's delay blitz is difficult to pick up.
- Quick-contain rushers off the edge have an advantage against offensive tackles in man protection.
- Strong versus any roll-out pass
- Strong push up the middle
- All receivers jammed off the line of scrimmage

Weaknesses:

- The pass defenders have no safety help.
- In a two-back formation, the back to the strongside may run a seam route and be unaccounted for.

46 Nickel Free Safety Zone Blitz

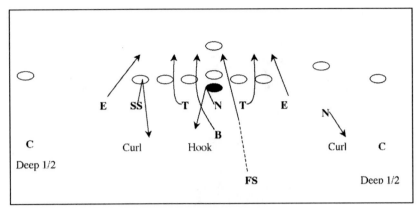

Diagram 10-10. 46 nickel free safety zone blitz

Situational Uses:

- Against a man-on-man (big-on-big) pass protection
- Against a team with a good tight end who is used in pass routes
- To force a hot throw
- When the back is expected to stay in for protection

Strengths:

- Six-man rush
- The free safety's delay blitz is difficult to pick up.
- Quick-contain rushers off the edge have an advantage against offensive tackles in man protection.
- Strong versus any roll-out
- Strong push up the middle
- All receivers jammed off the line of scrimmage

Weaknesses:

- The pass defenders have no free-safety help.
- Contain rushers must use a blitz-peel technique on a back who releases into a pass route.

46 Nickel Man Coverage with a Free Safety

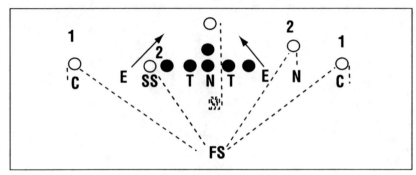

Diagram 10-11. 46 nickel man coverage with a free safety

Situational Uses:

- When double-coverage is desired on a particular receiver
- In a situation where an offense has a tendency to throw a post or dig to their "go-to" receiver
- Against man-on-man (big-on-big) pass protection
- Against a team with a good tight end who is used in pass routes
- Against a team that has one or more offensive tackles who can be beaten off the edge with a speed rush
- When the back is expected to stay in for protection

Strengths:

- Easily disguised
- Five-man rush
- Ability to use defensive-line games without affecting the pass coverage
- The free safety bracketing with either one of the corners or the nickel
- Quick-contain rushers off the edge have an advantage against offensive tackles in man protection.
- Strong versus any roll-out
- Strong push up the middle by the nose and defensive tackles collapses the pass pocket.

Weaknesses:

- No defender assigned to the quarterback for a quarterback throwback
- The offense may take advantage of a speed mismatch between the Mike and the single back.
- It may be necessary to help the Mike; the rush ends are taken out of their pass rush when using blitz-peel technique if the back releases to their side.
- Three pass defenders have no safety help.

46 Nickel Nose and Tackles Games

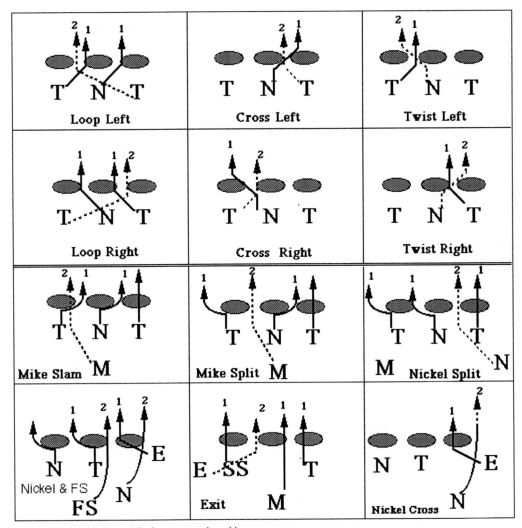

Diagram 10-12. 46 nickel nose and tackles games

Situational Uses:

- Against man-on-man (big-on-big) pass protection
- Against "zone-across" protection
- As a change-up

Strengths:

- Crossing action may free up a pass rusher by forcing an assignment error by an offensive lineman.
- Offensive line forced into difficult adjustments while on the move

- Quick-contain rushers off the edge have an advantage against offensive tackles in man protection.
- Offensive linemen may be caught "sleeping" when using these change-ups.
- The defenders may slant into a play.

Weaknesses:

- Seams may be created for a quarterback scramble.
- Seams may be created for a big run if a back gets past the line of scrimmage.

11

Even-Front Strategies Versus an Empty Backfield

Introduction to Defending Five-Receiver Formations in the Spread Offense

The empty backfield is one of the ways the spread offense can respond to defenses stacking the line of scrimmage. In the empty backfield, the quarterback is the only player in the backfield. The running backs are either replaced by receivers, or line up in receiver positions. In this instance, "empty" or "quads" formations are either four receivers to one side of the formation and one to the other side (often referred to as 4 x 1 sets), or three receivers to one side and two to the other (3 x 2 sets). The use of these five-receiver formations limits defenses, in most cases, to only three or four down linemen in the pass rush, because the rest of the personnel are needed in coverage. This situation gives quarterbacks time to set up in the pocket, opens up throwing lanes that would not exist against a normal pass rush, and lets receivers get into their routes and come out of their breaks.

A defense can play empty sets with two safeties (a "two shell"), one safety (a "three shell"), or no safeties. Zone, man, man-free, combination, and zone-pressure coverages can be used to defend these empty sets.

The diagrams detailed in Chapters 11 and 12 show the defense versus shotgun quads (4 x 1) formations. Furthermore, only quads to the left are diagramed. As such, the formation and accompanying strategies are equally effective versus quads to the right.

Neither chapter includes diagrams versus 3 x 2 sets. However, it is easy to apply the strategies shown versus 4 x 1 sets to the 3 x 2 sets. To play 3 x 2 sets, simply move a defender from the quads side to the opposite side of the formation and align him over the inside receiver. Almost all of the zone coverages shown versus quads do not have a flat defender to the single-receiver side. Therefore, when the offense moves a receiver from the quads side to the other side, thereby creating a 3 x 2 set, the defense should automatically place a flat defender to that side.

Many of the diagrams have a line drawn connecting a linebacker to the quarterback in the shotgun. This line indicates a "spy" technique by the linebacker. Thus, the defense dedicates one defender to the quarterback to take away his potential to run the ball on called run plays, or scramble runs. If the linebacker is not dedicated to the spy technique, he can either be used in coverage or included in the pass rush.

Even-Front Defenses Versus the Empty Backfield

The even-front defense has the ability to show a wide variety of coverage and pressure possibilities, including a no-safety look, a one-safety look, or a cover 2 shell. The primary emphasis in the following pages is on scheme rather than individual technique. Position alignments within the diagrams are not meant to be exact. The emphasis is not on creating a whole new defense with specific alignments, reads, and techniques. Rather, the goal is to offer strategies to defend the spread, using the alignments, reads, and techniques already taught in the defensive system. This approach is beneficial because it minimizes the need for new teaching and perfecting new techniques. For example, if a defense prefers to play press-man coverage, it can use the alignments and techniques specific to its program. The same reasoning applies to line and linebacker alignments and techniques in pass or run defense. Also, base personnel can be used for assignments in all of the diagrams in both Chapter 11 and 12. For example, defensive backs can be substituted for linebackers, and vice versa. Personnel should be played where they have the best chance for success when implementing the strategies detailed in Chapters 11 and 12.

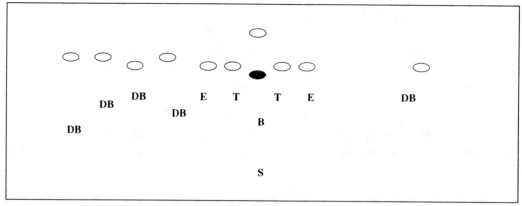

Diagram 11-1. 4-1-6 dime with one safety (or a 4-2-5 with a defensive back replacing an inside linebacker); the actual alignment would depend on the coverage and/or pressure call.

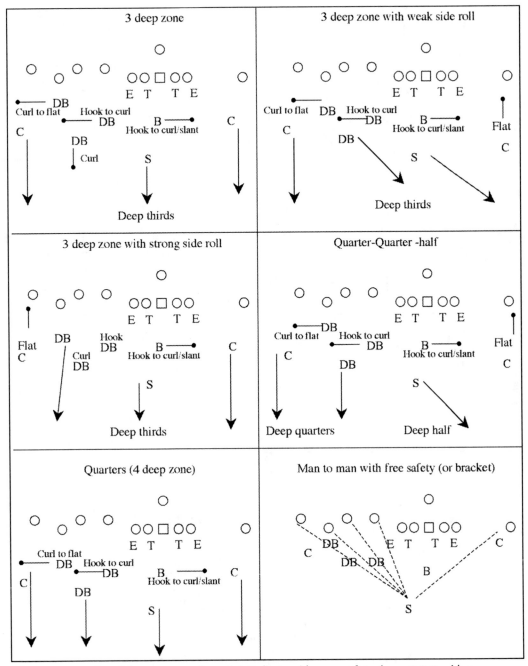

Diagram 11-2. Possible coverages in a 4-1-6 dime with one safety (or a 4-2-5 with a defensive back replacing an inside linebacker)

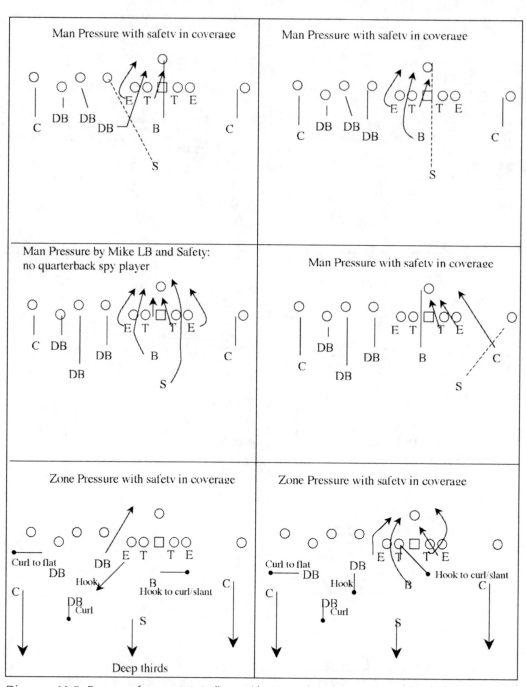

Diagram 11-3. Pressure from a 4-1-6 dime with one safety (or a 4-2-5 with a defensive back replacing an inside linebacker); an off-man technique or a press-man technique may be used.

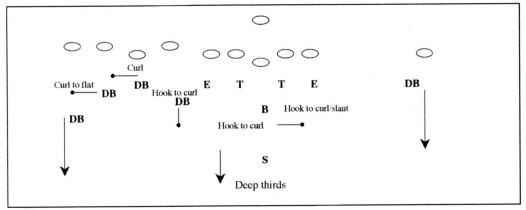

Diagram 11-4. Three-deep zone (or a 4-2-5 with a defensive back replacing an inside linebacker)

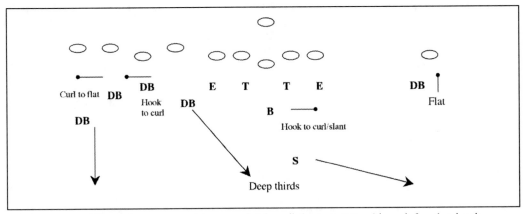

Diagram 11-5. Three-deep zone with a weakside roll (or a 4-2-5 with a defensive back replacing an inside linebacker)

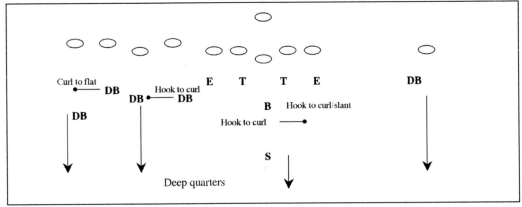

Diagram 11-6. Quarters coverage—four-deep (or a 4-2-5 with a defensive back replacing an inside linebacker)

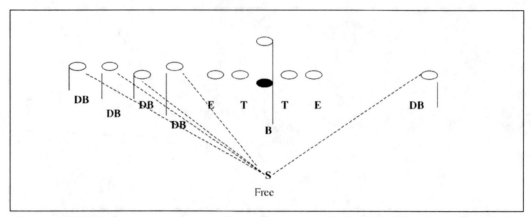

Diagram 11-7. Bracket-man coverage with a safety (or a 4-2-5 with a defensive back replacing an inside linebacker)

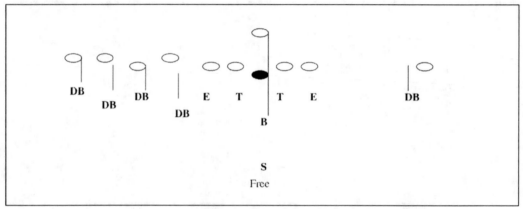

Diagram 11-8. Press-man coverage with a free safety (or a 4-2-5 with a defensive back replacing an inside linebacker)

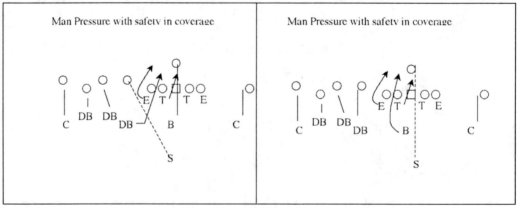

Diagram 11-9. Five-man pressure (or a 4-2-5 with a defensive back replacing an inside linebacker)

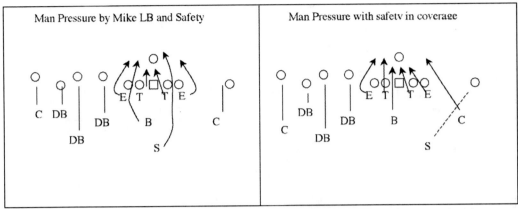

Diagram 11-10. Six-man pressure (or a 4-2-5 with a defensive back replacing an inside linebacker)

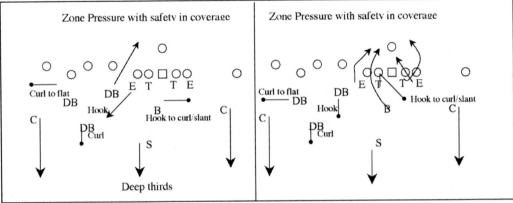

Diagram 11-11. Zone pressure (or a 4-2-5 with a defensive back replacing an inside linebacker)

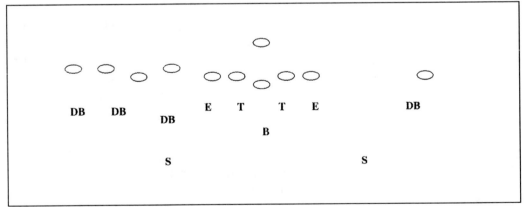

Diagram 11-12. 4-1-6 dime with a 2 shell—sample alignment; the actual alignment would depend on the coverage and/or pressure call.

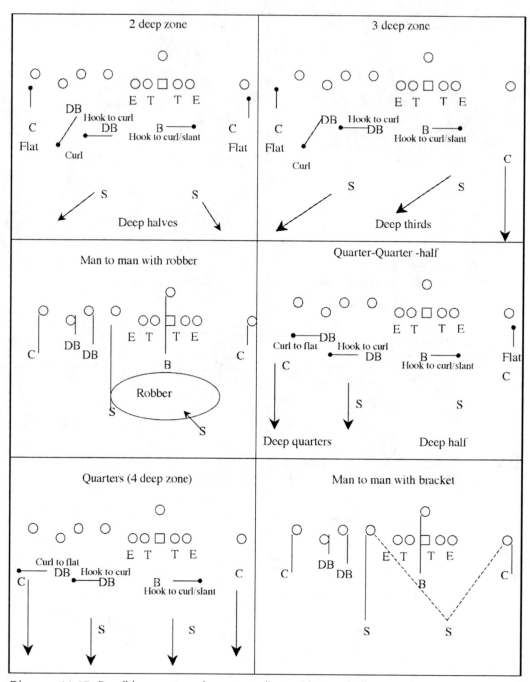

Diagram 11-13. Possible coverages in a 4-1-6 dime with a 2 shell

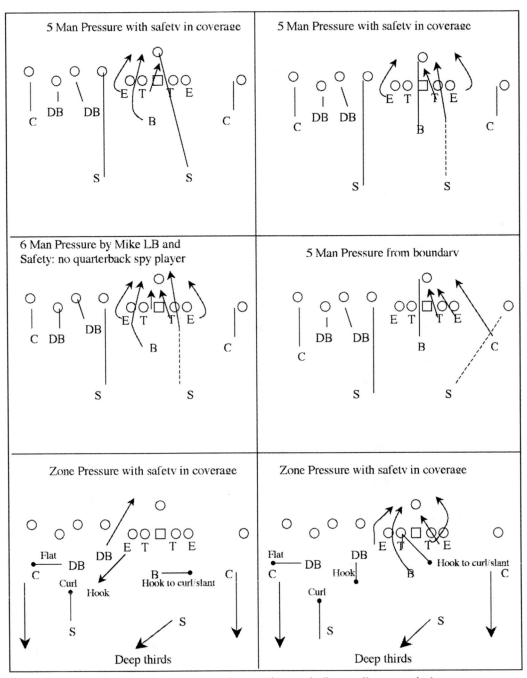

Diagram 11-14. Pressure from a 4-1-6 dime with a 2 shell; an off-man technique or a press-man technique may be used.

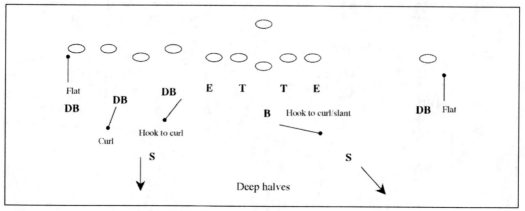

Diagram 11-15. Two-deep zone

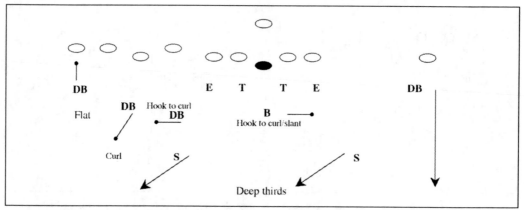

Diagram 11-16. Three-deep zone with a strongside roll

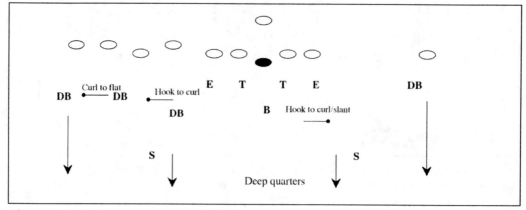

Diagram 11-17. Quarters coverage—four-deep

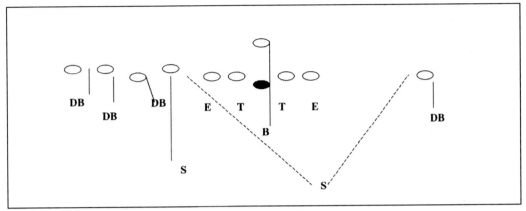

Diagram 11-18. Bracket coverage with a free safety

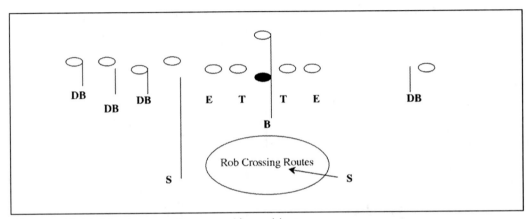

Diagram 11-19. Man-to-man coverage with a robber

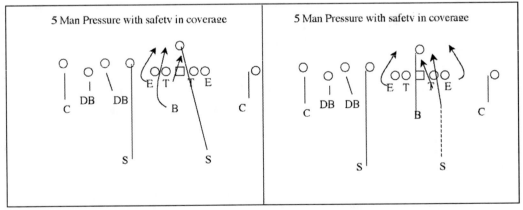

Diagram 11-20. Five-man pressure

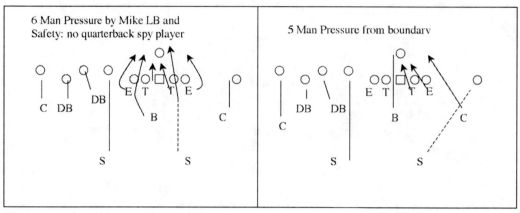

Diagram 11-21. Six-man pressure

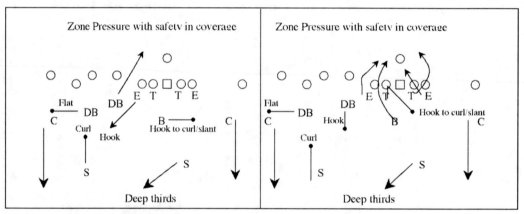

Diagram 11-22. Zone pressure

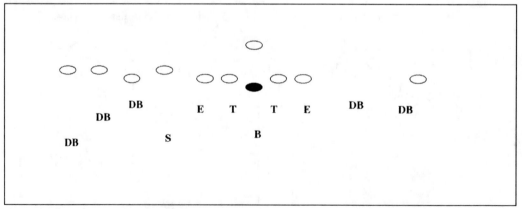

Diagram 11-23a. 4-1-6 dime with no safety—sample alignment; the actual alignment would depend on the coverage and/or pressure call.

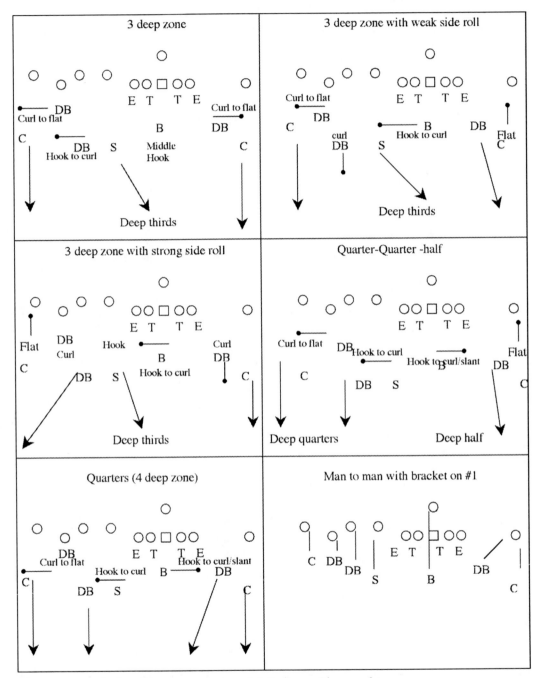

Diagram 11-23b. Possible coverages in a 4-1-6 dime with no safety

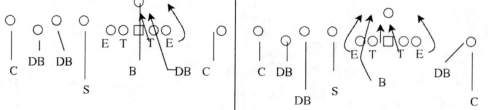

5 Man Pressure with safety in coverage

5 Man Pressure with bracket to single receiver

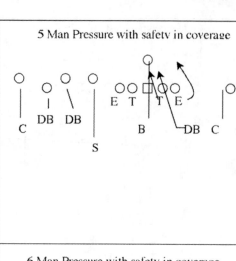

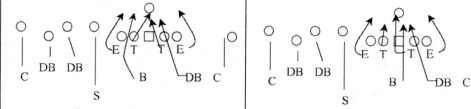

6 Man Pressure with safety in coverage

6 Man Pressure with safety in coverage

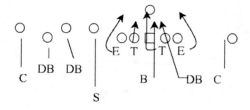

Zone Pressure with safety in coverage

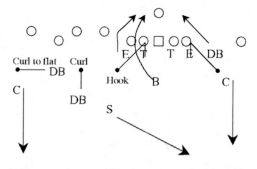

Diagram 11-24. Pressure from a 4-1-6 dime with no safety; an off-man technique or press-man technique may be used.

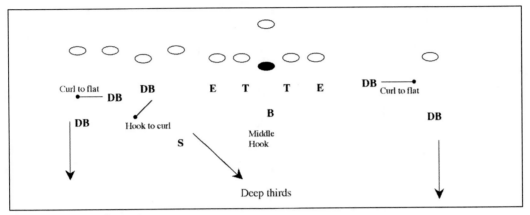

Diagram 11-25. Three-deep zone

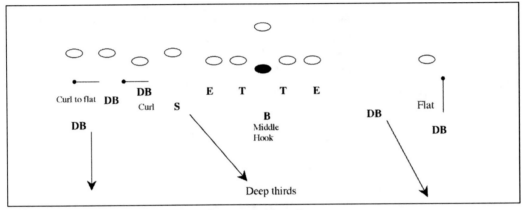

Diagram 11-26. Three-deep zone with a weakside roll

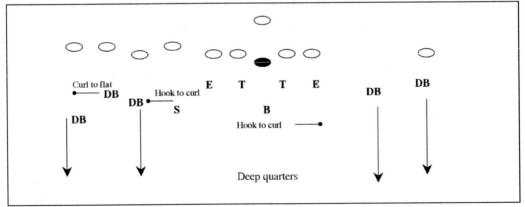

Diagram 11-27. Quarters coverage—four-deep

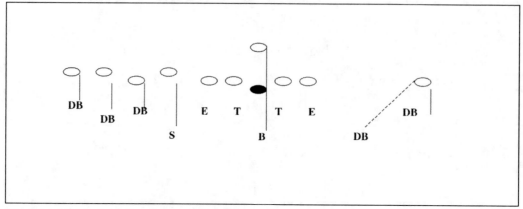

Diagram 11-28. Bracket coverage with no free safety

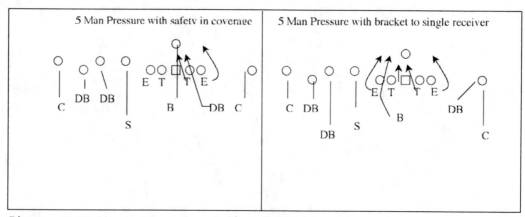

Diagram 11-29. Man-to-man coverage with no free safety

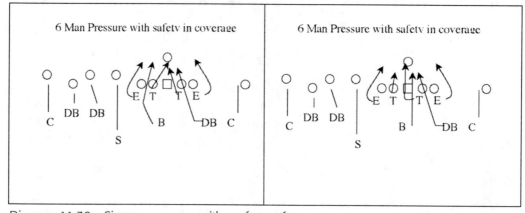

Diagram 11-30a. Six-man pressure with no free safety

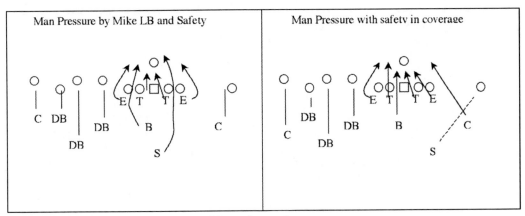

Diagram 11-30b. Six-man pressure with no free safety

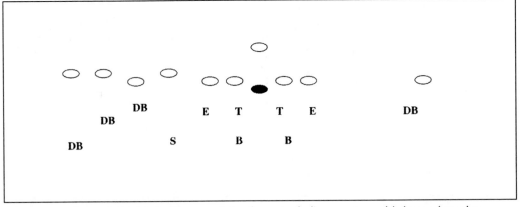

Diagram 11-31. 4-2-5 nickel with no safety; the actual alignment would depend on the coverage and/or pressure call.

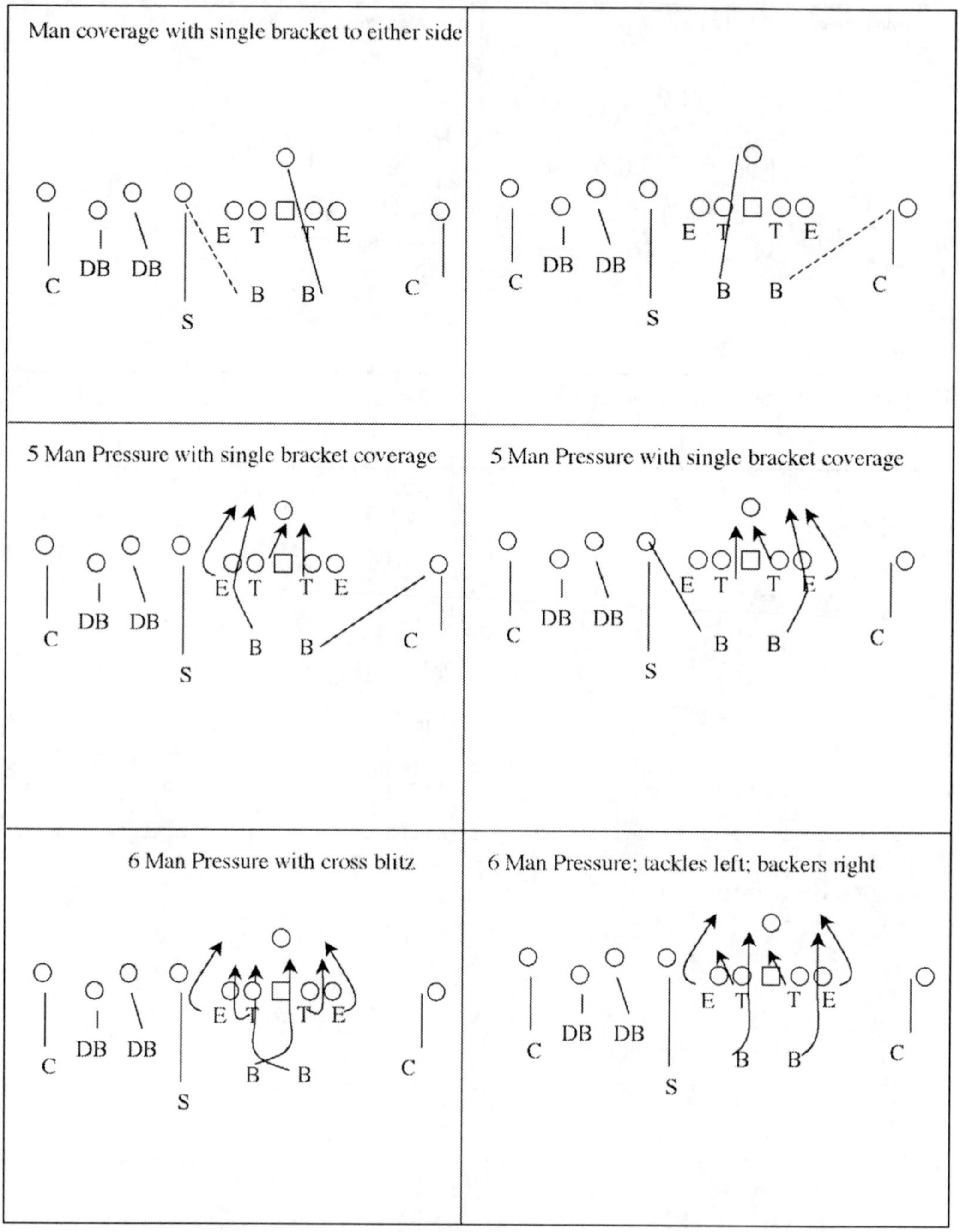

Man coverage with single bracket to either side

5 Man Pressure with single bracket coverage

5 Man Pressure with single bracket coverage

6 Man Pressure with cross blitz

6 Man Pressure; tackles left; backers right

Diagram 11-32. Pressure from a 4-2-5 with no safety; an off-man technique or press-man technique may be used.

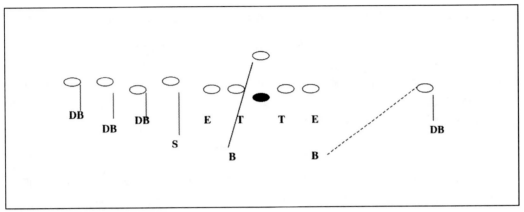

Diagram 11-33. Bracket coverage

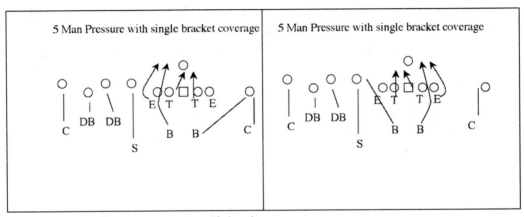

Diagram 11-34. Five-man pressure with bracket coverage

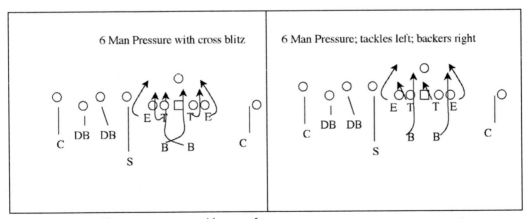

Diagram 11-35. Six-man pressure with no safety

Alignment Versus a Tight End in an Empty Formation from an Even Front

Adjusting to a tight end in a no-back set can be as easy as making no adjustment at all, or may require a change in alignment by one or more personnel. Likewise, a change in coverage is not required unless a specific adjustment is needed. The key is to make sure the defense is balanced against a set with a tight end, which is the basic rule when aligning against any offensive formation.

Some general guidelines for adjusting to a tight end include:

- Work within the philosophy of the normal defensive adjustments to a tight end.
- Do not allow the defense to be outnumbered to either side of the formation.
- If the tight end is likely to enter the pass pattern and a jam is required, a defender may be placed head-up on the tight end in order to prevent a free release.
- If the tight end may be used in protection, move the defensive end to an outside shade of the tight end to provide a better pass rush angle.
- If the tight end may be used in protection, and the defense wants to keep an end aligned on the tackle, send a quicker outside rusher (such as a defensive back or linebacker) to capitalize on a foot-speed advantage.

Very little difference exists when a tight end is utilized in a 4 x 1 empty set, or a 3 x 2 empty set. Diagram 11-36 shows a tight end in a 4 x 1 set. The same adjustments may be made versus 3 x 2 sets.

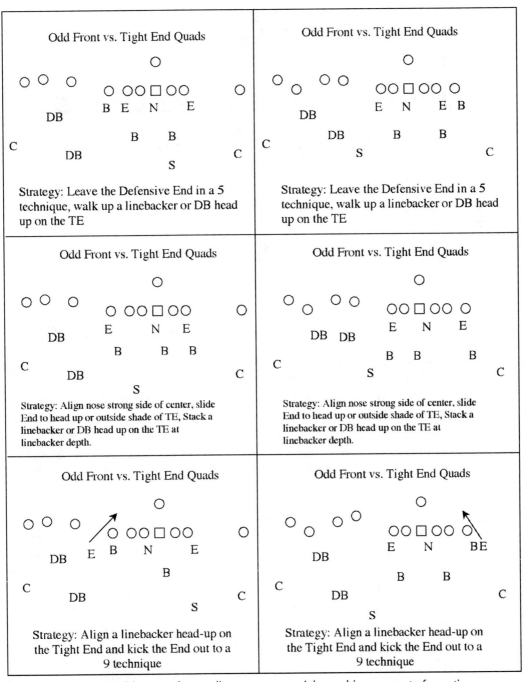

Diagram 11-36. Possible even-front adjustments to a tight end in an empty formation

12

Odd-Front Strategies Versus an Empty Backfield

Introduction to Defending Five-Receiver Formations in the Spread Offense

The odd front is an alternative to the even-front defense when defending the spread offense. The odd defense usually features a "3-2" dime or "3-3" nickel package that puts five or six defensive backs in coverage. In order to create a pass rush, the defense will stunt its down linemen and blitz two or three linebackers. The odd-front defense is effective because it allows teams to play a combination man/zone coverage with its five or six defensive backs, while creating pressure up front with a lot of movement from different angles. This movement creates confusion for blocking techniques and schemes.

The diagrams in this chapter are versus shotgun quads to the left. To implement quad strategies versus 3 x 2 formations, simply move a defender from the quads side to the opposite side of the formation, and align over the inside receiver. Almost all the zone coverage shown versus quads do not have a flat defender to the single-receiver side. Therefore, when the offense moves a receiver from the quads side over to the side (creating a 3 x 2 set), the defense should automatically place a flat defender to that side. In man coverage, this defender would be assigned the inside receiver on the two-receiver side, unless he is included in the pressure.

Similar to the previous chapter, the primary emphasis in this chapter is on scheme rather than individual technique. Position alignments within the diagrams are not meant to be exact. The objective is to offer strategies to defend the spread using the alignments, reads, and techniques already taught in the defensive system. Also, personnel should be placed where they have the best chance for success when implementing the strategies detailed in this chapter.

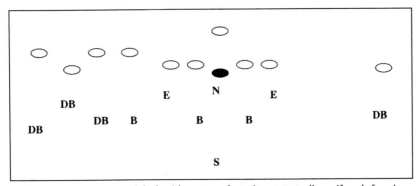

Diagram 12-1. 3-3-5 nickel with one safety (or 3-2-6 dime if a defensive back is substituted for the linebacker); the actual alignment would depend on the coverage and/or pressure call.

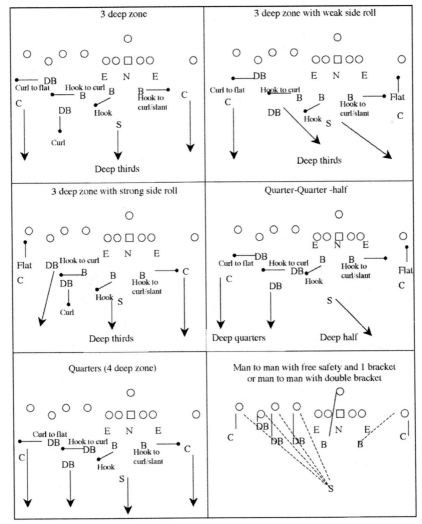

Diagram 12-2. Possible coverages in the 3-3-5 nickel with one safety

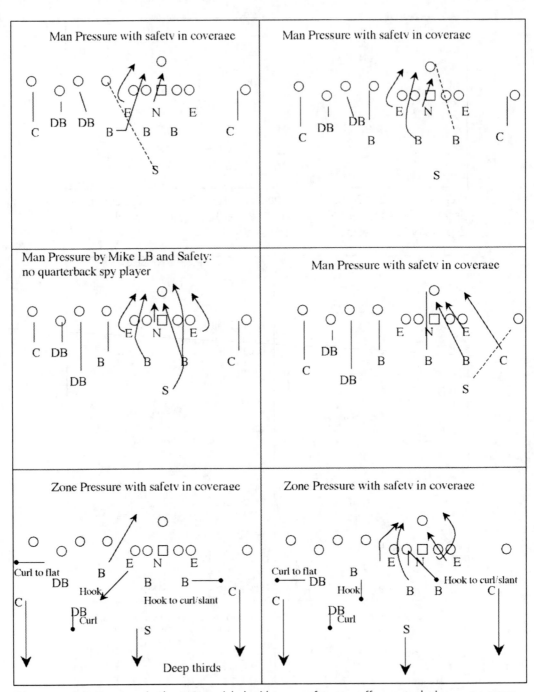

Diagram 12-3. Pressure in the 3-3-5 nickel with one safety; an off-man technique or a press-man technique may be used.

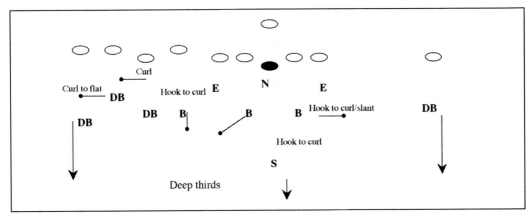

Diagram 12-4. Three-deep zone

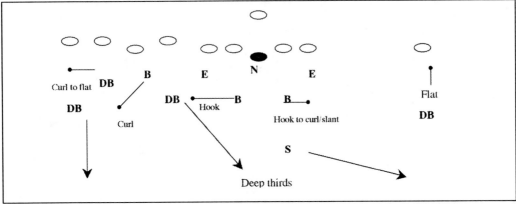

Diagram 12-5. Three-deep zone with a weakside roll

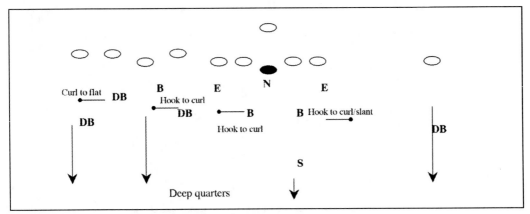

Diagram 12-6. Quarters coverage—four-deep

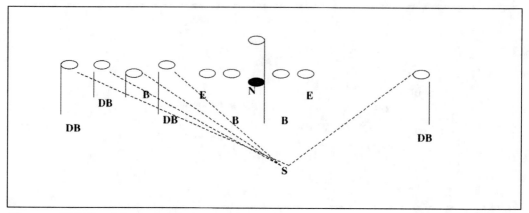

Diagram 12-7. Bracket man-to-man coverage

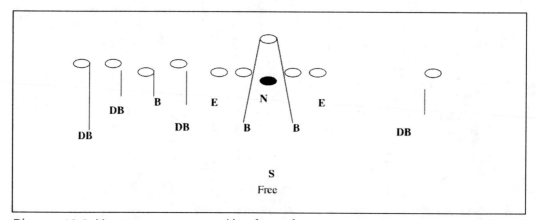

Diagram 12-8. Man-to-man coverage with a free safety

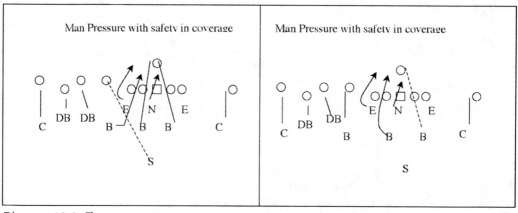

Diagram 12-9. Five-man pressure

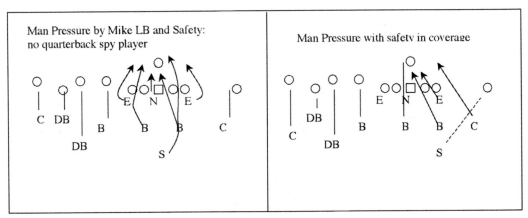

Diagram 12-10. Six-man pressure

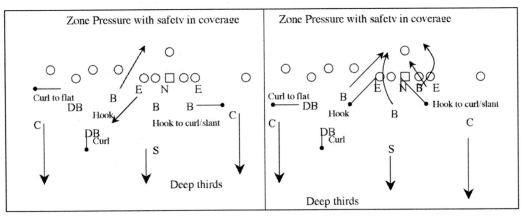

Diagram 12-11. Zone pressure

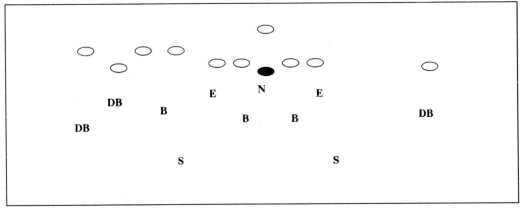

Diagram 12-12. 3-3-5 nickel with cover 2 shell (or for a 3-2-6 dime, substitute a defensive back for the left linebacker); the actual alignment would depend on the coverage and/or pressure call.

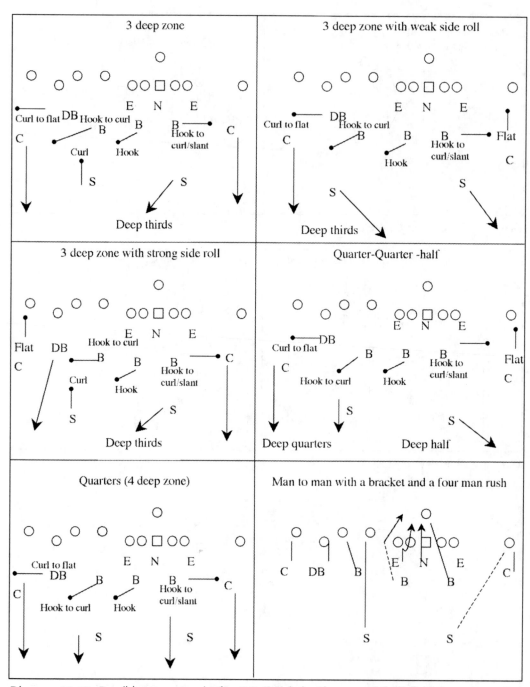

Diagram 12-13. Possible coverages in the 3-3-5 nickel with cover 2 shell (or for a 3-2-6 dime, substitute a defensive back for the left linebacker)

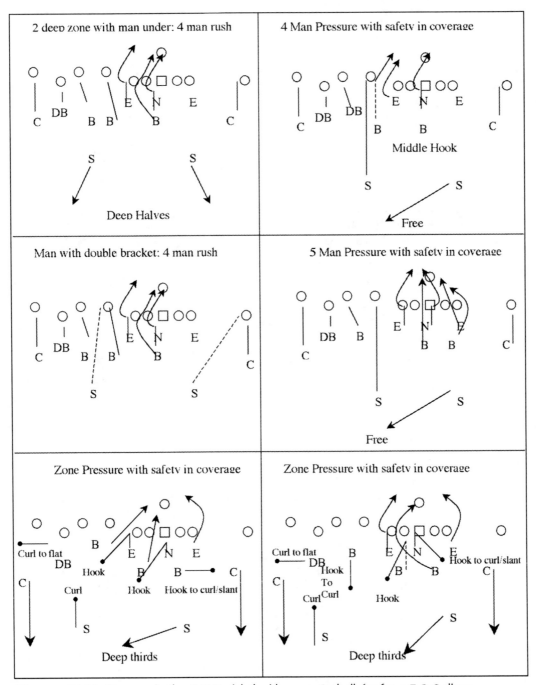

Diagram 12-14. Pressure in the 3-3-5 nickel with cover 2 shell (or for a 3-2-6 dime, substitute a defensive back for the left linebacker); an off-man technique or a press-man technique may be used.

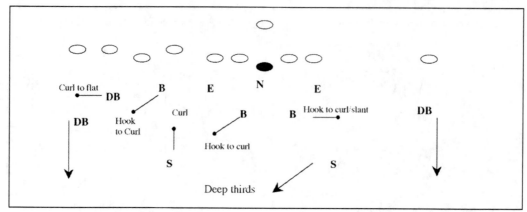

Diagram 12-15. Three-deep zone with cover 2 shell (or for a 3-2-6 dime, substitute a defensive back for the left linebacker)

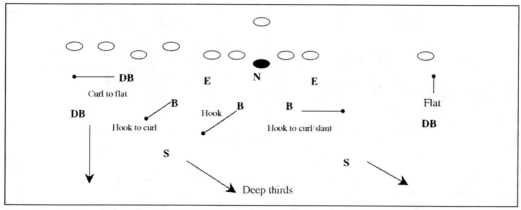

Diagram 12-16. Three-deep zone with a weakside roll

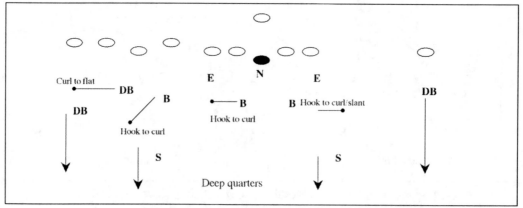

Diagram 12-17. Quarters coverage—four-deep (or for a 3-2-6 dime, substitute a defensive back for the left linebacker)

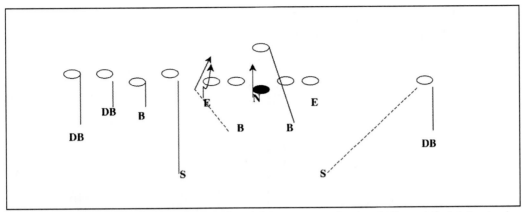

Diagram 12-18. Man coverage with bracket (or for a 3-2-6 dime, substitute a defensive back for the left linebacker)

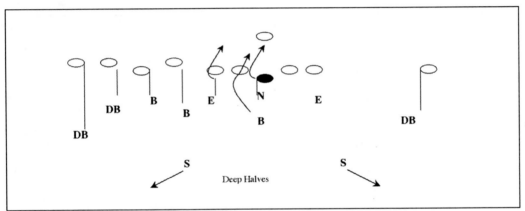

Diagram 12-19. Two-deep man under (or for a 3-2-6 dime, substitute a defensive back for the left linebacker)

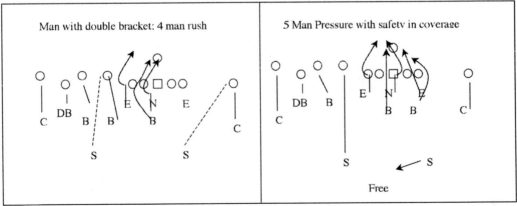

Diagram 12-20. Other strategies (or for a 3-2-6 dime, substitute a defensive back for the left linebacker)

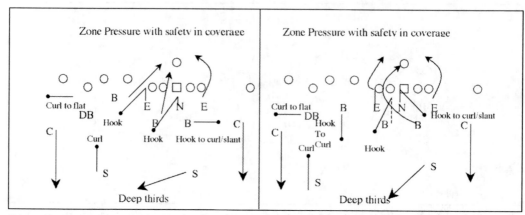

Diagram 12-21. Zone pressure (or for a 3-2-6 dime, substitute a defensive back for the left linebacker)

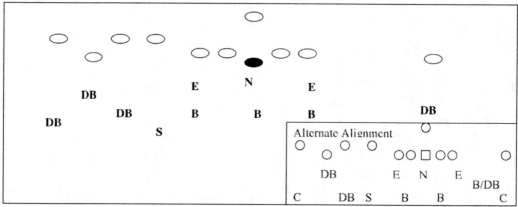

Diagram 12-22. 3-3-5 nickel with no safety (or for a 3-2-6 dime, substitute a defensive back for a linebacker); the actual alignment would depend on the coverage and/or pressure call.

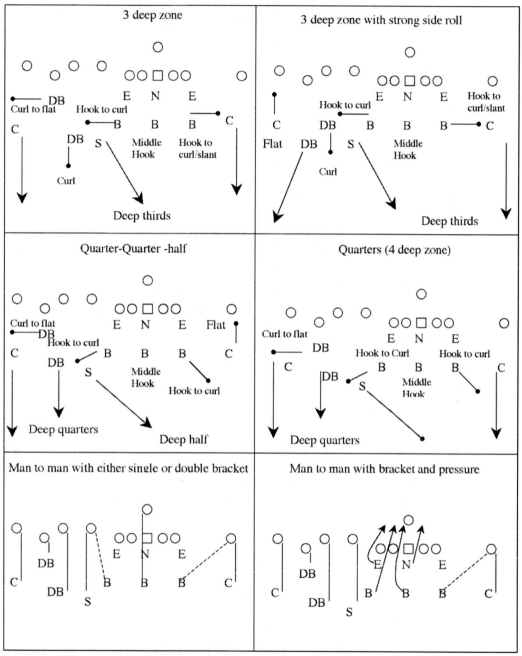

Diagram 12-23. Possible coverages (or a 3-2-6 when a defensive back is substituted for a linebacker)

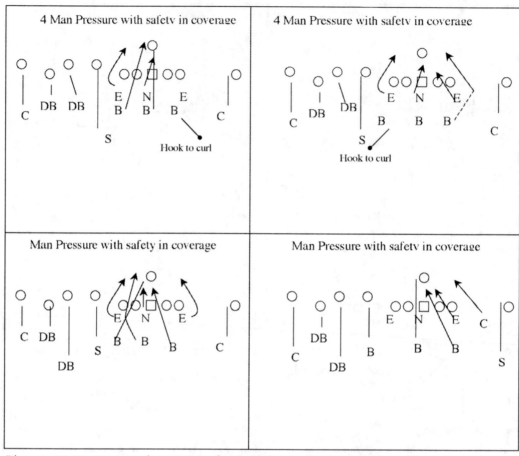

Diagram 12-24. Pressure (or a 3-2-6 when a defensive back is substituted for a linebacker; an off-man technique or a press-man technique may be used

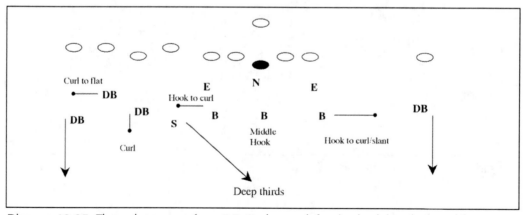

Diagram 12-25. Three-deep zone (or a 3-2-6 when a defensive back is substituted for a linebacker)

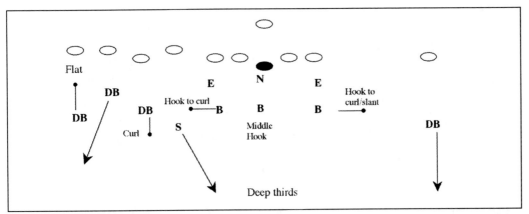

Diagram 12-26. Three-deep zone with a strongside roll (or a 3-2-6 when a defensive back is substituted for a linebacker)

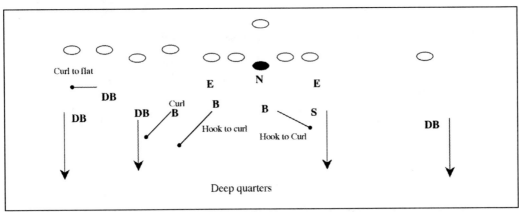

Diagram 12-27. Quarters coverage—four-deep (or a 3-2-6 when a defensive back is substituted for a linebacker)

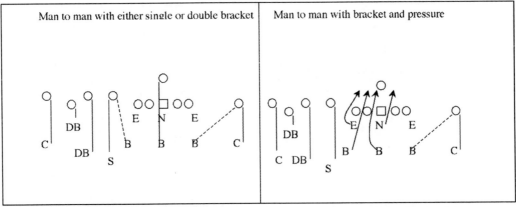

Diagram 12-28. Bracket man-to-man coverage (or a 3-2-6 when a defensive back is substituted for a linebacker)

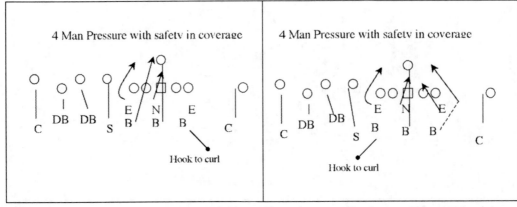

Diagram 12-29. Man-to-man coverage with pressure (or a 3-2-6 when a defensive back is substituted for a linebacker)

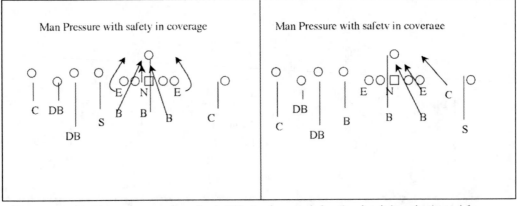

Diagram 12-30. Five-man pressure (or a 3-2-6 when a defensive back is substituted for a linebacker)

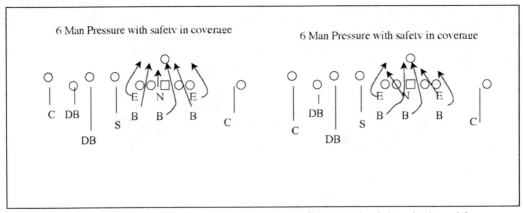

Diagram 12-31. Six-man pressure (or a 3-2-6 when a defensive back is substituted for a linebacker)

Alignment Versus a Tight End in an Empty Formation with an Odd Front

When the defense is deploying a 3-2 or 3-3 front versus a tight end within a no-back set, it is important to make the proper adjustments or the offense will have a five-to-three advantage on the line of scrimmage.

Adjusting to a tight end in a no-back set may require a change in alignment by one or more personnel. Likewise, a change in coverage need not exist unless a specific adjustment is needed. The key is to make sure the defense is balanced against a set with a tight end, which is the basic rule when aligning against any offensive formation.

Some general guidelines for adjusting to a tight end include:

- Work within the philosophy of the normal defensive adjustments to a tight end.
- Do not allow the defense to be outnumbered to either side of the formation.
- If the tight end is likely to enter the pass pattern and no jam off the line is desired, it may not be necessary to make any adjustment at all.
- If the tight end is likely to enter the pass pattern and a jam is required, a defender may be placed head-up on the tight end in order to prevent a free release.
- If the tight end may be used in protection, move the defensive end to an outside shade of the tight end to provide a better pass rush angle.
- If the tight end may be used in protection, and the defense wants to keep an end aligned on the tackle, send a quicker outside rusher (such as a defensive back or linebacker) to capitalize on a foot-speed advantage.

Very little difference exists when a tight end is utilized in a 4 x 1 empty set or a 3 x 2 empty set. Diagram 12-32 shows a tight end in a 4 x 1 set. The same adjustments may be made versus 3 x 2 sets.

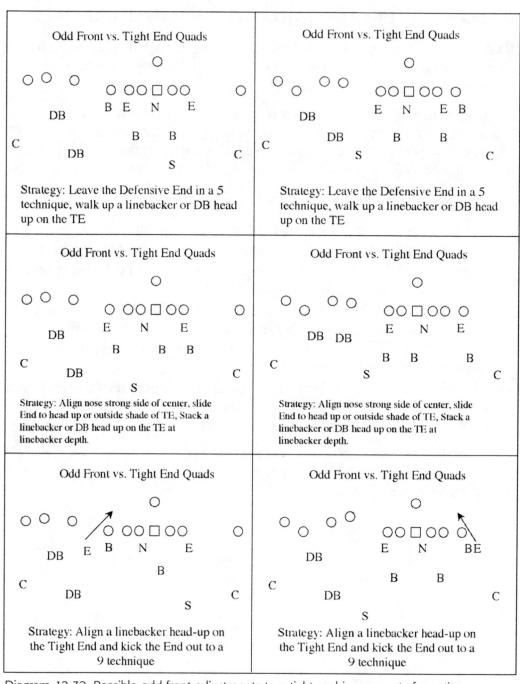

Diagram 12-32. Possible odd-front adjustments to a tight end in an empty formation

13

Fusing Bracket Coverage and Pressure Concepts Versus the Spread Offense

Coaches should think of a bracket/pressure package as a toolbox from which defensive coordinators can pick and choose the parts of the scheme that may be most beneficial to their team's defensive needs and personnel. Rather that concentrate on individual technique, the primary focus of this chapter is on the strategy of fusing bracket coverage with pressure concepts within the 3-3 stack defense, both with one safety (a 3 shell) and two safeties (a dime and a safety comprising a 2 shell). The package provides a wide variety of "specific tools" that can be employed to address specific offensive strategies. In order to facilitate a sound understanding and installation progression of fusing these concepts, it may be helpful to compartmentalize the three key elements of the package: the pressure component, the coverage component, and the bracket component.

The Pressure Component

In order to eliminate new teaching, therefore saving valuable practice time, this chapter utilizes the same pressure concepts that were used in the base pressure package that was previously detailed from a one-safety look (a 3 shell). Several of the base pressure concepts are illustrated in Diagram 13-1.

The task of having coaches choose which pressure to employ should be a function of their opponent's pass-protection schemes, as well as their own team's specific strengths concerning its ability to execute a pressure defense. In that regard, among the general rules for incorporating a pressure defense that have proven effective over the years, are the following:

- Avoid inside pressure vs. 90 protection; the inside blitzers are not likely to be a factor.

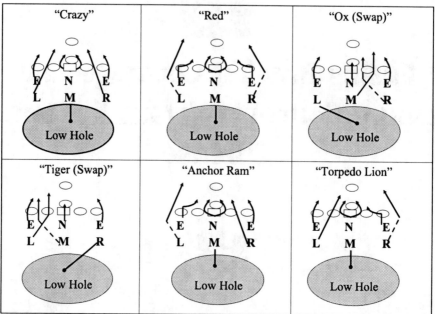

Diagram 13-1. Examples of base pressure concepts

- Use gap exchanges between linebackers and down linemen vs. man-protection schemes.
- Use overloads vs. man-protection schemes.
- Use outside pressure vs. slide protection (send one more blitzer than the offense can block to the slide).
- Create mismatches vs. big-on-big protection (the best pass rusher should be assigned vs. their weakest link).
- Utilize zone-pressure and zone-blitzes vs. 90 protection when a quarterback tends to make predictable hot reads.
- Don't re-invent the wheel; utilize pressure that the opponent hasn't picked up well, based on scouting.

The Coverage Component

The coverage component is the most complex and time-consuming factor in a bracket/pressure package, in terms of teaching and installation. The first element of this component is man-to-man coverage. This element involves defenders playing press-man coverage, both with and without safety help in this package. If defense already employs man coverage in its base scheme, then it will have little, or no, new teaching to do when installing the package.

Some teams utilize both inside and outside press technique and off-man technique in their bracket/pressure package. In those situations, because each defender may be called upon to employ both inside and outside press technique (depending on the bracket call), those teams typically will work on their techniques in pre-practice during one-on-one passing drills and during scheduled practice time during pass skeleton. With regard to man-to-man coverage, some teams also employ trail-man technique as well.

In reality, if a team doesn't already utilize some man-coverage techniques, it may find the time that it must invest in order to teach man-coverage prohibitive. For that reason, many teams often start teaching man technique to their defenders during the spring, and continue to work on perfecting it during 7-on-7 passing contests during the summer.

The second element of the coverage component involves teaching the dime's assignment in the two-safety shell-look. From a two-shell contour, the free safety will be aligned on one side, and the dime back (who is inserted for the least-capable man-coverage defender) will align opposite—thus, a two-shell look. The dime can be assigned various techniques to execute, depending on the call. He may be a deep-half defender, a bracket defender, a low- or high-hole defender, or an off-man defender for a blitzing linebacker (refer to Diagrams 13-2a through 13-2f).

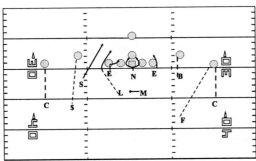

Diagram 13-2a. Dime's assignments in "dime lock" adjuster for the blitz

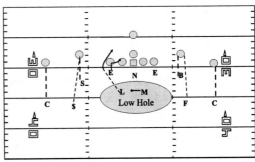

Diagram 13-2b. Dime as a bracket defender

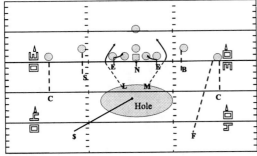

Diagram 13-2c. Dime's assignments in "dime lock" hole

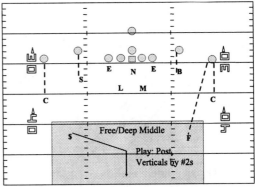

Diagram 13-2d. Dime as a deep-middle player

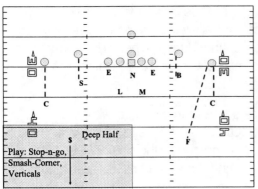
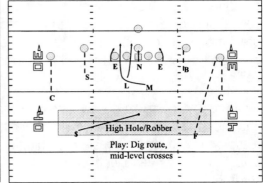

Diagram 13-2e. Dime as a deep-half player   Diagram 13-2f. Dime as a high-hole player

As Diagram 13-2 illustrates, utilizing all of the possible techniques for the dime would necessitate teaching each technique against specific routes. Teaching the techniques most likely to be included in a particular week's game plan can maximize the defense's productivity. Unless a team is playing an opponent that throws the ball 60 times a game, it is not likely that it would use all of the possible techniques for a dime on a weekly basis.

Bracket Component

The bracket component refers to the specific technique used by two defenders (a free safety and a corner or a linebacker; or a dime and a corner or a linebacker) and the various calls associated with the package. Diagram 13-3 provides a graphic overview of inside and outside bracket technique, with the safety responsible for one side of the passing tree and the other defender (corner or linebacker) responsible for the other.

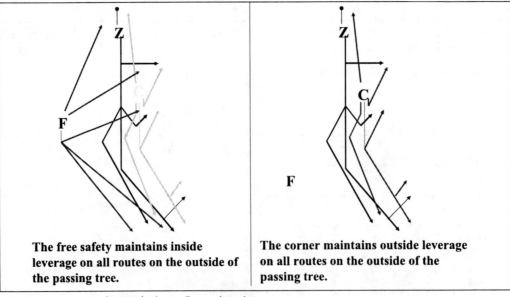

The free safety maintains inside leverage on all routes on the outside of the passing tree.

The corner maintains outside leverage on all routes on the outside of the passing tree.

Diagram 13-3. Bracket technique (in and out)

Most teams begin teaching the bracket component in the spring, and carry on through the summer. The effort involves walking the defenders through each route, and showing them the proper spatial relationship to the receiver that is expected. Coaches want each defender to overplay his half of the tree and anticipate which route is coming, based on the scouting report and the stem of the receiver's route. For example, the corner is expected to overplay the out route and not worry about an "out-and-up," because the safety is responsible for the second break. Likewise, the safety should overplay the post route, knowing the corner is in position and expects the second break for the post-corner. These routes are typically run during practice without balls being thrown in order to get the defenders comfortable reading the routes. Most teams work on the bracket technique extensively over the summer in an attempt to identify and correct technique errors. Over the summer, most teams also work on identifying motion and formations, which will invoke coverage checks, and will force the secondary to check out of bracket coverage from day one, so that it is undertaken with confidence should the necessity arise during the season.

Specific Schemes Within the Package

"Duo" is one of the basic schemes in the bracket/pressure package. It is most effective when the back is included in the protection scheme (Diagram 13-4).

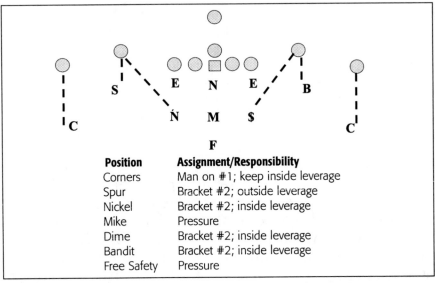

Position	Assignment/Responsibility
Corners	Man on #1; keep inside leverage
Spur	Bracket #2; outside leverage
Nickel	Bracket #2; inside leverage
Mike	Pressure
Dime	Bracket #2; inside leverage
Bandit	Bracket #2; inside leverage
Free Safety	Pressure

Diagram 13-4. the "duo" bracket/pressure scheme

Diagram 13-5 illustrates some of the pressure that can be used in the duo scheme. In this instance, "Ohio" is a term for outside pressure, while "Indiana" is a term that signifies inside pressure. In the example, the nose engages the center briefly, and then drops as a low-hole player, defending quick crosses and draws. The call can be tagged to bring the pressure from the right or left, field, or boundary. For example, if the defense wants outside pressure from the field, the call would be "Duo Ohio." Duo signifies double-bracket utilized on the number 2 receivers and single coverage on the outside. Although this coverage is best used when the single back is employed in the protection scheme, a simple way to safely assign coverage to him would be to teach the defensive ends a peel technique, wherein they peel off their pass rush and cover the back on any flare by the back, and/or assign the nose to pick up the back on a back's release between the tackles.

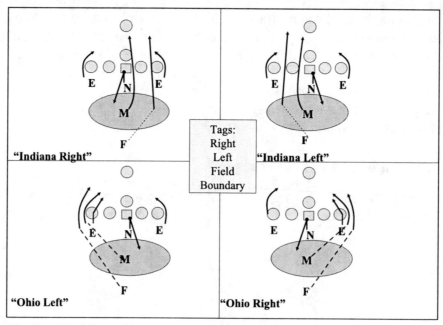

Diagram 13-5. Examples of duo pressures

"1 Bracket" Scheme

Another scheme within the bracket/pressure package from the base defense (three-shell) that can be utilized is the "1 bracket" scheme. In this scheme the safety and a corner are assigned to bracket a pre-determined receiver. Diagram 13-6 illustrates a scenario in which the receiver to be double-covered was wearing number 89. In this situation, the huddle call would be "1 bracket #89 (blitz desired)." The hole player is assigned to defend draws, quick crossing routes, and quick-hitting runs. On the other hand, since the offense could easily not come out in a vanilla 2-by-2 set, appropriate checks need to be in place. Table 13-1 details some possible adjustments to trips.

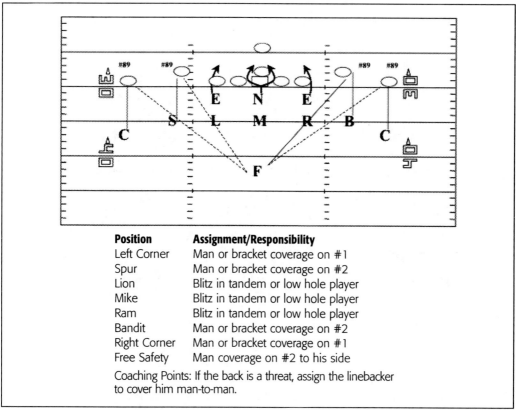

Position	Assignment/Responsibility
Left Corner	Man or bracket coverage on #1
Spur	Man or bracket coverage on #2
Lion	Blitz in tandem or low hole player
Mike	Blitz in tandem or low hole player
Ram	Blitz in tandem or low hole player
Bandit	Man or bracket coverage on #2
Right Corner	Man or bracket coverage on #1
Free Safety	Man coverage on #2 to his side

Coaching Points: If the back is a threat, assign the linebacker to cover him man-to-man.

Diagram 13-6. the "1 bracket #89" scheme

Formation/Motion	Check
Trips/Motion to Trips	Play it
Empty/Motion to Empty	Ram or Lion man on #3, Tiger or Ox
Bracketed Player in the backfield	Play it with in-out alignment adjustment

Table 13-1. Examples of possible "1 bracket" formation/motion checks

Linebacker Play in 1 Bracket ## Pressure

Diagram 13-7 illustrates each of the three stacked inside backers' responsibility for six separate blitzes. Notice in each blitz, two of the three linebackers will blitz and the remaining linebacker will be responsible for the "low hole" and be responsible for any quick hitting run plays that may get by the other five "box" defenders. The linebacker responsible for the hole will be responsible for denying the first shallow crossing route by any receiver attempting to cross the field. If the quarterback rolls out or scrambles, he may be assigned to mirror the quarterback, much like a player assigned a spy technique.

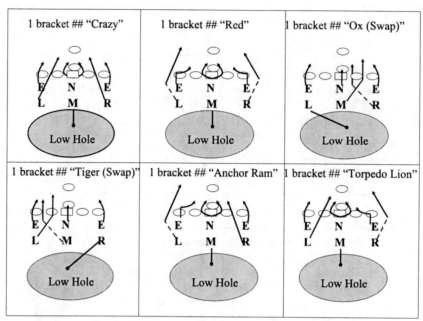

Diagram 13-7. Linebacker assignments in "1 bracket ## pressure"

Numbers Package

Another integral part of the bracket/pressure package is the "numbers" package (Diagram 13-8). Teams have been utilizing this package for years with their even-front and 3-4 packages. In fact, many teams have adapted this package to their 3-3 stack. It is executed from a two-shell look (three down linemen, two linebackers, four man-to-man defenders, and two safeties). For teaching purposes, receivers are identified by number from outside-in. in other words, in a 2-by-2 set, the two receivers to the defensive left, the Z would be identified as #1, and the Y identified as #2. On the opposite side, the X, or outside receiver, is identified as #1, and the inside receiver, the H, is identified as #2. If the offense went empty, utilizing a 3-by-2 set, then the inside-most receiver would be identified as #3. In the numbers package, a double-bracket is utilized on predetermined receivers, based on the pre-snap alignment. For example, teams may want to bracket the outside most receivers in a formation, the receivers identified as the #1s. In that situation, the dime and left corner would bracket the number 1 (Z) on the defensive left, and the free safety and right corner would bracket the #1 (X) on the defensive right.

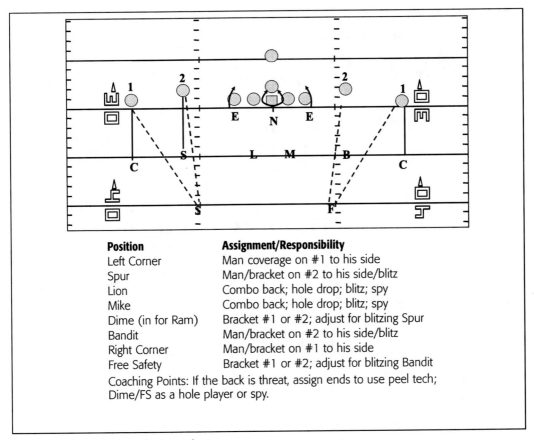

Position	Assignment/Responsibility
Left Corner	Man coverage on #1 to his side
Spur	Man/bracket on #2 to his side/blitz
Lion	Combo back; hole drop; blitz; spy
Mike	Combo back; hole drop; blitz; spy
Dime (in for Ram)	Bracket #1 or #2; adjust for blitzing Spur
Bandit	Man/bracket on #2 to his side/blitz
Right Corner	Man/bracket on #1 to his side
Free Safety	Bracket #1 or #2; adjust for blitzing Bandit

Coaching Points: If the back is threat, assign ends to use peel tech; Dime/FS as a hole player or spy.

Diagram 13-8. The numbers package

Accordingly, double-covering the number 1s would be called "dime numbers "11." The first digit assigns the left safety (dime) to double a particular receiver, while the second digit assigns the right safety to double a specific receiver to his side. Therefore, if a team wants to double both slot receivers, they would call "22." The dime can also be assigned to be a hole player, cover for a blitzing defender, or play deep-half, as was discussed previously. In this regard, some of the possible combinations are illustrated in Diagrams 13-9 through 13-12.

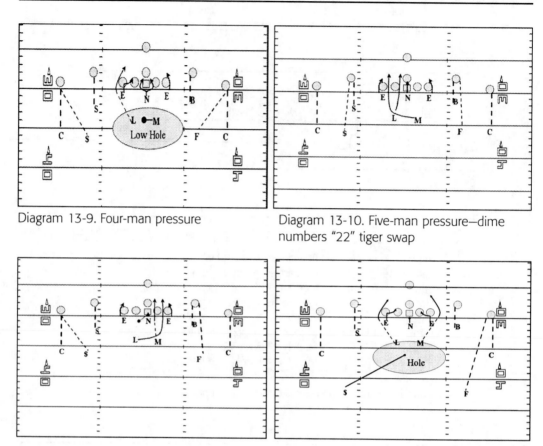

Diagram 13-9. Four-man pressure

Diagram 13-10. Five-man pressure—dime numbers "22" tiger swap

Diagram 13-11. Five-man pressure: numbers 12 ox (swap)

Diagram 13-12. Dime numbers hole 2 red

Given the space limitations that exist in a book of this scope, it is not feasible to list all of the bracket/pressure possibilities. Dozens of pressure and bracket combinations are possible in this package. For the same reason, the number of possible adjustments to trips and motion has also received relatively limited attention in this text. On the other hand, coaches need to be aware of how to make adjustments to their team's bracket/pressure package when the situation calls for them. A safe adjustment on motion to trips, for example, is to keep the bracket on to the 1-receiver side, break the bracket to the trips side, and assign the safety to man-up on the motion man, all the while maintaining the pressure. Still another safe adjustment is to check to a base zone if concern exists of a mismatch favoring the offense. An adjustment to empty can be handled many ways, one of which is to break the bracket to the three-receiver side and assign the safety to that side to cover the back. Coaches who prefer to keep the double-bracket on can have their team adjust to the third receiver to one side with one of the remaining two inside linebackers and either keep the pressure on with the remaining inside linebacker or check out of the pressure and drop him as a low hole player. The key is to have more than one adjustment per formation or motion.

About the Author

John Rice is currently the defensive coordinator at Santiago High School in Corona, California, a position he assumed in 2009. He has been a high school football coach for over 25 years, and has served as a head coach, as well as a position coach and coordinator both offensively and defensively in a career that has included stints at two large-school state championship-level programs. In 2001, in his first season at national power Louisville Trinity High School, John helped guide the Shamrocks, as their defensive coordinator, to their 13th large-school state championship. In 2000, he served as the defensive backs' coach at large-school state runner-up Denver Bear Creek High School.

He has coached high school football in California, Colorado, Kentucky, and Indiana in a career that has included a prolific body of work, including authoring two books, *Coaching Nickel and Dime Defenses*, and *Defending the Spread Offense*, as well as being featured on over 30 instructional coaching videos on a wide variety of both offensive and defensive topics. He has also published articles in both *Gridiron Coach Magazine* and *American Football Coach Magazine*. In addition, he has been a frequent speaker at the renowned Glazier Football Clinics and was a featured presenter at the prestigious Ohio Football Coaches annual clinic in 2007.